Forgiving the Unforgivable

"The Cry of the Daffodils"

Kitty Chappell
62 N. Soho Place
Chandler, AZ 85225
480-857-6674
www.kittychappell.com

To my brother Chuck and my sister Chris, who can say with me:

"Don't let evil conquer you, but conquer evil by doing good."

Romans 12:21

Kitty Chappell

I Can Forgive If I Want To

Vocatio Publishers
Phoenix, Arizona

Vocatio Publishers
3841 E. Chandler Blvd, Suite # 106-106
Phoenix, AZ 85048, USA
e-mail: ceo@vocatio.us
www.vocatio.us

This book was formerly published under the title of *Sins of a Father—Forgiving the Unforgivable*.

ISBN 978-0-9792342-3-1

Table of Contents

PART TWO

Acknowledgements

Each of us is an artist. Our thoughts, words, and actions are the brush strokes used to help paint not only our self-image, but those of others. I thank God for the trustworthy artists in my life, friends and relatives who through the years have applied warm-colored words of encouragement and praise, layer by layer, upon the canvas of my mind—a craft executed in love.

I am grateful for the godly ministers, Sunday school teachers, and fellow Christians in my life who "walked their talk," leaving golden footprints across my mind.

I thank God for one exceptional artist—my ever-praying maternal grandmother. Her glowing words of affirmation in my dark environment made me feel I had value, regardless of my performance. In the early years of my mind, she faithfully placed diamond-studded Scriptures into its every nook and cranny, then covered them with prayer. They lay there, ready to shine with the brilliance of understanding when the light of Christ flooded my soul at the age of fourteen.

I thank God also for the negative strokes, the black and blue bruises on my soul, the razor sharp edges of actions and remarks that cut to the core of my mind's canvas, letting the bright red from my wounds bleed through. Without the penetration of ugly-colored experiences, there would have been no crimson to seep through and blend with the darker colors to form God's perfect color of purple compassion.

I am grateful that nothing is wasted in God's economy. He has helped me to use the brush strokes of good and evil alike, friends and foes, to help paint my character into a self-image worth viewing—that of a joyful overcomer.

Special, heartwarming thanks go to the dear ones listed below:

Joan Englander—The reporter who first wrote my story in her Ojai, California, newspaper column in 1982. Meeting her was divinely orchestrated—a meeting that set into motion a chain of events that is still at work.

Gerry King—My sweet friend and area representative for Stonecroft Ministries. After she read Joan's article, she encouraged me to become a speaker to Christian Women's Clubs and After-Five Christian Women's Business and Professional Groups. As a result, for more than twenty-five years I have shared the good news with thousands of women throughout the U.S. that they, too, can become overcomers.

Betty Arthurs—a fellow writer, as well as other dear friends in the Tuesday's Children Christian Writer's Group. With fear and trepidation I handed Betty my first chapter (the only one I had written) for her "absolutely honest" opinion. Had there been even the slightest sign of negative body language on her part, another layer of doubt would have been added to my already fearful mind that this book would be boring—and I probably would have shelved the idea. But her spontaneous response of "This is awesome!" splashed bright strokes of hope in my heart, and so I continued.

Etta Mae Pickens—My fiercest prayer warrior. At just the right moments, when I felt like giving up, the phone would ring and I'd hear her sweet voice reminding me that she was praying for me every day.

Shawna Bedal—I appreciate so much Shawna's invaluable help with Scripture research.

New Hope Publishers—who published the original edition of this book under the title of *Sins of a Father, Forgiving the Unforgivable.* I am forever indebted to them.

Vocatio Publishers—President and CEO Piotr Waclawik's enthusiasm in publishing this updated version is contagious. I am eternally grateful for his faith in this book and its message.

Pat Harris—My dearest friend of many years (I can't tell you how many because she swears she's not that old) has been my strongest supporter.

Jerry Chappell, My Late Husband—For forty-seven wonderful years he was my greatest admirer and supporter. I am thankful he didn't leave me during the writing of the first edition of this book—and grateful for his patience which was sorely tried at times. Once he ventured into my office, despite its warning sign that read, "Disaster Area," and timidly asked, "Honey, are you ever going to the store again?"

Introduction

Who hasn't been hurt by someone, somewhere, at some time? Who hasn't felt the sting of injustice, the emptiness of rejection, and the soul-gnawing presence of hate and resentment?

While not every individual has experienced abuse in the strongest sense of the word, each of us has felt abused and mistreated and has succumbed to self-pity at one time or another. But beware! Self-pity is the stuff that the victim mentality is made of. If allowed to ferment, age, and grow, self-pity can create a prison in which its victims suffer damage far greater than that inflicted by any perpetrator—a prison that fosters bitterness, not betterment.

This book is about surviving and overcoming. There are millions of survivors, but few overcomers. What is the difference between a survivor and an overcomer? Survivors live through their heartbreaking circumstances but never get beyond their pain. They live but they are not alive.

They remain trapped in their victimhood, blaming others for their problems. Some robe themselves in self-pity and drag their hurts behind them like dirty, tattered security blankets— defying anyone to step on them. Others blast fiery charges of hate into innocent bystanders—either with words or with bullets. And at the end of the day, they curse their misery as they stare blankly through the bars of a prison fashioned by their own flawed thinking. They do not see the key hanging by their window—the key to freedom.

Overcomers have also survived heartbreak and pain, but they have discovered the key within their grasp and use it wisely. They unlock the doors of their past and use its stumbling blocks as stepping stones to freedom. They exchange their tattered robes of self-pity for clean and practical garments of accountability. They walk in strength and grace. They rejoice in the fresh air of their freedom and the sunrise of their joy, for they know that neither heartache nor tragedy will ever again hold them prisoner.

While this book contains heartache, horror, and disappointment, it is about hope and overcoming. It was not written by a group of detached observers of pain, or by a professional panel who discussed and debated theories as to how those who have been deeply wounded should deal with their pain. Nor is it a "somebody done me wrong but I survived anyway" book. It is a story of God's power and grace.

This book was written by an individual who was born into an environment of violence, experienced the pain of abuse and the ravages of rage and resentment, yet emerged not as a mere survivor, but as a victorious overcomer.

As a speaker to women's groups for over twenty-five years, it became increasingly clear to the author that most of us need help in letting go of our hurts. We need assistance in developing accountability to God and man if ever we hope to overcome our pain and become all God intends us to be—and deep in our hearts, we long to be.

Part One

Chapter One

Sins of a Father

The two caskets stood side by side on their stands. One, laden with flowers, proclaimed from its satin banner, “Our beloved mother and sister.” My stepmother. The second bore no banner. Just a single red rose, a solitary symbol of remembrance for my father.

Heavy with grief and guilt, I wept silently, thoughts churning. *Have I failed again? Could I have prevented this? Should I have shot him long ago as I had planned? If I had, none of this would have happened.*

Dad had always been violent. My earliest memories were of him beating my mother as I cringed in a corner. Holding my hands over my ears did not shut out her screams.

My brother Charles was born when I was three years old, and our sister Christine when I was seven. I quickly assumed the mother role, not only for my siblings, but also for our young mother, a mere fifteen years older than I.

As a toddler, Charles often crawled out of his cot during the night and sleepwalked toward the front door. In wide-eyed terror, whimpering like a frightened puppy, he clawed at it with quick dog-like strokes—futile attempts of a tiny boy subconsciously trying to escape his environment.

It was my responsibility to get Charles back onto his cot quickly, since Mom feared any movement on her part might awaken Dad. But sometimes I slept too soundly and failed to reach him in time. Angered by his disruption of sleep, Dad would bound out of bed, grab Chuck's frail body, and beat him with a leather belt, mumbling, "I'll teach the little ..... to wake me up!"

"Clyde, please don't, he's just a baby," Mother cried out, grabbing at Dad's arms.

"Shut up, Esther! Stay out of this!"

"But he doesn't know what he's doing. He's sleepwalking," Mom begged.

"Then this will wake him up!" Dad snarled.

Mom's attempts to intervene always ended the same. She was knocked to the floor where she lay frozen in fear. She knew further attempts to help Charles would result in Dad beating him even harder. I flinched as I heard the thick leather strap slapping against Charles' frail, bony frame. His screams pierced the stillness of the night and stabbed my heart with deeper guilt.

I lay there motionless, afraid to breathe. Once I heard the rhythmic sound of Dad's deep breathing, I crept to Charles' cot and stroked his wet face. My tears blended with his as I whispered, "I'm sorry I didn't wake up in time."

~

"Happy birthday, honey. You are now a teenager!" Mother announced with a smile, eyes glowing with pride. "Make a wish and blow out your candles."

I stared at the double-layer chocolate cake covered with fluffy white frosting. Pink flowers with tiny green leaves danced around its sides, while thirteen pale green candles, placed evenly around the cake top, guarded the flowers below. *Happy Birthday, Kitty,* the center of the cake greeted in cherry pink script letters with tiny matching flowers dotting every i.

"It is so beautiful, Mom, thank you."

Birthdays were special to our mother. Never had she missed baking us our favorite cake, and as far back as I could remember she had encouraged us to invite our friends over for a party. But not this time.

I closed my eyes and made my wish.

I wish my father were dead!

As special as turning thirteen was for me, I had declined a party at the last minute because I didn't want Mom to be embarrassed. Her right eye was swollen and black, with prominent bruises on her right jaw. I knew she would lie to cover up for Dad, and I couldn't stomach that.

Despite Mother's gaiety, the scene was somber. I glanced at Charles, whom we now called Chuck, hunched over the table, head bowed, resting on his knuckles, elbows rigid. I couldn't tell if his eyes were closed or if he was just staring at the patterns on the oilcloth. To my left sat six-year old Chris, golden hair shining (she had given it extra brushes for this special occasion). Her eyes danced as she eyed the cake, eagerly waiting for me to cut the first slice, knowing she would get the next piece. Like a graceful butterfly, she waved her delicate arms, fanning the smoking candles before Mother and I gathered them onto a saucer.

Dad's place was empty. He had stormed from the table earlier, following his usual threats of punishment. He took advantage of meal times, when we were all together, to reprimand us of any misdeeds, perceived or real. Who could eat after receiving a pronouncement of the punishment that would be forthcoming once the meal was over? Birthdays were no exception.

"Hmmm, hmmm, it is so good! This is your best cake yet, Mom!" I exulted, glancing toward Chuck. I smacked loudly as I licked frosting from my fingers, and placed the first moist slice onto my plate. I watched for Chuck's reaction since I knew chocolate was also his favorite. He lifted his head slowly and fixed his gaze on the edible vision beckoning from the center of the table. By the time I had placed an extra thick slice on his plate, the sparkle had returned to his sad blue eyes.

~

Dad's cruelty, and inconsistency in showing it, confused us. While he appeared to love some of our pets, he would without apparent provocation kill others.

Late one Saturday afternoon I arrived home from babysitting all day for a neighbor down the street. The delicious aroma of frying chicken bombarded my hungry senses as I opened the door. "Yum, that smells so good!" I called out to Mom as I walked into the kitchen. Mom didn't turn and welcome me with her usual smile, nor did she answer. She just stood there at the stove, her back to me, rigid.

"Mom? What's the matter?"

Finally she turned a tear-streaked face to me and said, blinking hard, "Your little sister needs you."

"Why? What's wrong?" Mom chewed her bottom lip, as if to keep from crying, and nodded toward Chris's room.

For a moment, I stood outside her door, listening to the soft sobs on the other side.

"Honey, it's me," I said, pushing the door open gently. Chris sat on the floor with her head in her arms on the side of her bed. She wore her favorite ruffled pinafore, the one that was so tedious to iron. She always tried, however, not to dirty it. I was surprised, when she jumped up, to see long streaks of dark red stains splashed across its front.

Is that blood? My heart pounded.

"What happened, honey, are you hurt?"

Suddenly Chris threw her arms around me, hugging me hard. Her body shook as she sobbed into my hair, "My Henrietta is dead!"

Oh, no. Not her favorite little pet!

A friend of the family had given each of us a dyed "Easter chick" the previous spring. They were the cutest, cuddliest creatures we had ever seen. Pink, blue, and orange fluff balls of joy that brightened our days. Chris immediately named her chick Henrietta, and they became inseparable. A month later, Chris proudly demonstrated how she had trained Henrietta to come on demand. Each day, after arriving home from school, Chris rushed to the back door, threw it open, and called out, "Henrietta! Come, girl."

Henrietta always came quickly and rubbed her feathered face against Chris's ankles, weaving excitedly in and out between them, until Chris scooped her up in her arms and they rubbed their faces together.

"Only the soul of a child can understand the deep love bond between a pet and the heart that cherishes it," I had written in my diary that day. "All creatures respond to love and every child needs the opportunity to express love."

I thought of how Chris had poured all the pent-up love she carried for Father, who would never return it, upon a small creature who always returned it in full. "My Henrietta," she often murmured in joy, stroking the satiny red feathers of her beloved pet, holding her close to her face. Henrietta, with closed eyes, obviously enjoyed those moments, for she never struggled to escape. It was with reluctance that she let Chris place her in the coop with the other two pet chickens at sundown where she would be safe for the night.

"What happened?" I asked, pushing Chris away enough so I could see her face.

I was unprepared for her response. Chris's eyes narrowed. Through clenched teeth and trembling lips she hissed, "Daddy killed her." She started shaking as the pent-up pain spilled from her overloaded heart. "He killed all of them, our pets. Yours, Chuck's, and my Henrietta! And he made me watch! He wouldn't let me leave."

Oh, no! How could he!

Tears trickled onto Chris's hair as I held her close, both of us trembling. "I'm so sorry, honey," I cried, holding her tightly. But she needed to talk. She had to verbalize her story of horror.

"I went outside to let Henrietta out so I could play with her, but Daddy was already there, standing by the coop. He said he was waiting for me. Told me to stay where I was, that he wanted me to watch something. Then he grabbed Blossom, your pet chicken, yanked her out of the cage, and closed the door. He held her up high and began wringing her neck. I started crying. I turned to run back inside, but he yelled, 'You stay right where you are. Don't you move!' Blossom was flopping around on the ground, dying, when he reached in and grabbed Chuck's chicken. When he did the same thing to Bessie, I knew he was saving my Henrietta for last."

Chris broke into loud sobs as she relived her tragic experience. I held her tightly, but there was no stopping her avalanche of pain. Its momentum pushed her headlong into the path of her story.

"I started screaming, 'Daddy, please don't hurt Henrietta!' But he wouldn't stop. I knew Henrietta was scared— she'd just watched her sisters die! And she was flapping her wings trying to get out of the cage. I didn't want to watch Henrietta die, too, but when I turned Daddy yelled again, 'You move one step and I'll beat you within an inch of your life!' He reached into the back of the cage and grabbed Henrietta by the head. One of her wings got caught on the side of the opening, and she squawked. I knew it hurt her, but Daddy just yanked harder until she was out. He jerked her up and down by the head, swinging her around and around, moving closer and closer to me so I had to watch. Then he threw her to the ground so hard that her little neck broke completely off. Blood spurted everywhere, even on my dress."

My heart ached and my throat burned from trying not to cry. *Poor little Chris—and she is so frightened at the sight of blood!*

"I started screaming louder but Daddy wouldn't let me move. 'Shut up!' he yelled, 'And don't close your eyes. It's not good for you kids to get so attached to things. So you watch!' Then he just stood there, smiling, while Henrietta's body kept flopping all around. I saw her little head lying in the grass, eyes still open, as if she had to watch too. I jumped when her body brushed against my legs, and Daddy laughed. I kept jumping around, stomping the ground hard, and trying to get the blood off me. I wanted to die. And Daddy just laughed harder!"

Emotionally spent, Chris buried her face in my chest and sobbed quietly, her breath catching every so often. I sat on the side of the bed with Chris huddled in my lap, my arms wrapped around her. I rocked her side to side in stoic silence. What could I say that could ease her intense pain?

Suddenly, fresh horror intruded my numb heart as a new realization pummeled my mind. *Oh, no! No wonder Mom was upset! Mom, who nurtures every injured wild bird we drag in back to health, and who loves anything with feathers on it, was forced by Dad to prepare and cook our pets! How terrible for her! And how will we ever get through the evening meal!*

A deathly pall hung over the supper table as we picked at our food. Only our father seemed to relish every bite, smacking loudly, slurping the grease from his fingers. Not even with threat of a beating would Chris touch the piece of chicken set before her. To distract Dad's wary eyes from her every movement, the rest of us ripped our meat apart, spreading it around on our plates with exaggerated motion, but not eating it. We nibbled at our vegetables while Chris moved her fork slowly through her mashed potatoes and separated her green beans.

Fortunately, Dad didn't notice that Chris wasn't eating.

Chris was finally allowed to leave the table when she started to throw up. As she ran for the bathroom, Dad called loudly after her, "This is the best chicken dinner I ever ate!" Then he laughed. I had experienced hate for my father prior to this, but nothing prepared me for the repulsion that seared my soul. While Dad pushed a pile of bones onto a side plate, I placed my hands quickly out of sight under the table where they doubled into tight fists. Inwardly, I screamed in rage, *How I hate you, Father. Some day I'm going to kill you!*

~

By the time I was 14, hate for my father was full-blown. I felt trapped and helpless. I often awoke exhausted from recurring nightmares in which my hands were tied behind my back and I was ordered to do something. "But I can't, my hands are tied!" I cried out. Nameless voices kept demanding that I do simple tasks that I couldn't do because my hands were tied. Many times I was awakened by my groans and heard my voice pleading, "But I can't, I can't." I dreaded going to sleep.

I finally realized that no matter how much I wanted to, I could not protect my family. Though I daydreamed of ways for us to escape, I knew it was impossible. Dad had warned us, "Don't you go mouthing off to anyone about things that's none of their business, or I'll put you all out of your misery."

Dad felt secure in our small Texas town where he was well liked. "No jury would ever convict me," he bragged. "I'd just plead temporary insanity." No one, including my closest friends, suspected the truth. They had no idea of the heartache we experienced behind the closed doors of our rose-covered house and well-trimmed lawn. To them, I was just an ordinary happy-go-lucky teenager with no worries other than what clothes to wear or which boy to date.

So picture-perfect did our lives appear that some of my friends expressed open envy. "You are so lucky, Kitty!" a classmate remarked one day. "Your mother is young and pretty, fun to be around, and your dad is the most handsome man I know—such gorgeous blue eyes and wavy brown hair. I am so envious! I wish I were you."

"Don't ever wish you were someone else," I said brusquely, taking her by the shoulders and shaking her. "Be thankful you are who you are and for the life you live." She looked at me strangely as tears filled my eyes before I turned and quickly walked away.

I hid my fear and hate carefully behind my smile and sense of humor, but I knew I couldn't live this way much longer. Something had to be done. But what? What choices did I have?

I was born during the mid-1930s and grew up in a time when our nation still reeled from the effects of the Great Depression. There were no shelters for battered women and children, and no agencies to provide financial aid or free legal counsel. The prevailing attitude of abused women at that time was the one expressed by my mother when she said, “Decent people don’t air their dirty laundry in front of others.”

Besides, what could an outsider do? We were on our own.

I was frustrated. I sought reasons for my father’s abusive behavior, but none were apparent. He wasn’t an alcoholic who would go on a binge and mistreat us, for he rarely drank. The few occasions I recalled his coming home tipsy from too many beers, he was so docile we weren’t afraid of him. I found myself wishing he would drink more.

I also found myself wondering why my mother married him, and especially at such a young age. Very soon I would learn the answers, but they would only fuel my desire to do away with my father.

CHAPTER TWO

The Unsuspecting Bride

One weekend following my fourteenth birthday, Mom and I were in the back yard trimming dead flowers from her prized bearded iris plants. The late afternoon sun highlighted the translucent petals and turned them into brilliant splashes of color. Deep purple, blue, amber, and bright golden hues filled the air with their sweet fragrance as a sudden playful breeze blew across the yard.

"Mom, why did you marry Dad when you were so young?" I asked, moving the bucket closer to her so she could deposit her pile of trimmings.

She didn't answer.

"Your mom and dad were great parents, and you got along well with your brothers and sister. I know you were poor because of Grandpa's crippled arm, and it must have been hard to go from place to place working crops, but you were happy. Why would you want to leave your parents and marry at the age of fourteen? I wouldn't dream of getting married now."

Still no answer.

"And why would Granny let you?"

Mom straightened up from her bent position, leaned backward on her knees, rubbed her back, and began answering my questions.

"I was introduced to Clyde right after we moved to Oklahoma, and he started coming over and talking to me. He was a handsome, confident eighteen year old, and I was flattered. Here was this catch-of-the-town showing an interest in me, a shy girl who had barely turned fourteen."

"What do you mean, catch-of-the-town?"

"Well, that's what everybody called him. And I'd seen how other girls hovered around him. Your granny wouldn't let him date me, said I was too young, but he kept coming over. He was charming and relentless in his efforts to convince your granny that she should let us date. She finally told him he could go to church with us if he wanted to and sit next to me, but he still couldn't take me out alone on a date. Our family never missed a church service and pretty soon neither did Clyde."

"Well, if Granny wouldn't even let you date him at fourteen, how did you end up marrying him at that age?"

Mom fell silent. With furrowed brows she sought the right words for her explanation. I snipped some dead blossoms from the plants further out into the bed and waited.

I heard Chuck and Chris laughing with their friends next door. *I love to hear them laugh,* I thought. *They certainly don't get to do a lot of that here. As much as we love each other, seems like all we kids do is argue.* The thought bothered me, for I was older and I felt I should set a better example. But I just couldn't help myself sometimes, and that made me feel even more irritable.

My legs were stiff. As I rose to stretch, a mockingbird flew over my head, loudly warning me not to venture near the chinaberry tree where she nested.

"Mom?" I finally asked, picking up my snippers and kneeling again into the flowerbed.

"This may sound strange," she said, reaching for a tall iris, "but I didn't know I was getting married."

I whirled to face her, mouth open, eyes wide. Before I could respond, she added, "That is, not until we all stood before the justice of the peace."

"You're kidding! How on earth could you not know you were getting married?"

We both rose to a sitting position. Mom smoothed her skirt out on the grass, tired of it being tucked between her legs, and said, "I didn't know it at the time, but Clyde had told your granny that he wanted to marry me. He said we were so madly in love that if she and your grandpa didn't sign for me and allow us to get married, then we would elope. He said he wasn't sure of where we would go next, nor when your granny and grandpa would see us again."

"You would do that? Just elope, not knowing if or when you'd see your parents again?"

"Of course not. As I said, I didn't know he had told Mom that."

"I don't understand. Why on earth would Granny let him bully her that way? She would stand up to the devil himself! And why would she agree to something as important as your marriage without even discussing it with you?"

"I guess your dad was so smooth and convincing— had all the plans made, even bought me a new dress, though it was much too big for me—that your granny assumed I was in on it and that was what I wanted. All of her lady neighbors had been raving about how great Clyde was, telling her, 'Mrs. Watson, that young Clyde sure would be a fine catch for little Esther. Handsome, hardworking, and everybody loves him. Why, any mother in this town would give her right arm to have him for a son-in-law!' "

"But you were so young!"

"Lots of teenage girls married back then, and with their parents' blessings. I think the main reason your granny let me get married, though, was because my older sister, your Aunt Martha, was giving them fits. She went through a sudden rebellious spell, just went wild—drinking, partying, staying out all night with disreputable guys. It was during that time, when my parents were totally distracted and beside themselves with worry about Martha, that Clyde told them we were getting married in a week."

"But didn't Granny even talk with you about it?"

"It all happened so fast and so many things were going on—Martha's rebellion, them trying to work the crops. I think she assumed it was a done deal and so they just went along with it. And, maybe deep inside, they thought I'd be safe if I married a nice young man. One thing I know for sure is that your granny has grieved herself almost sick ever since for letting me get married."

Poor Granny. How many times have I heard her say to me, "Till my dyin' day I'll never forgive myself for letting little Esther marry your father!" *But how could she know he was such a rotten apple?*

"So, how did it happen? When did you finally realize you were getting married?"

"When your dad gave me the new dress, which he'd said was okay with your granny for me to keep, and which I didn't know would be my wedding dress. He said it was for me to wear on a special occasion very soon, when we would take an all-day trip to the county seat. He said he wanted me to wear it then and look pretty for him. In those days, wedding dresses were rarely the white, fluffy things girls wear now—we just wore the prettiest dress we had. So this could have been any special-occasion dress.

"I remember how excited I was when the following Saturday we all piled into your Uncle Vernon's old Ford coupe, your dad and I sitting in the rumble seat, and drove to town. It was only when the county clerk started asking questions that I realized we were there for my wedding."

"Why didn't you say something?"

"By that time I was absolutely nuts about your father, and I thought, 'Well, I love him, so why not?' "

I couldn't believe what I was hearing. "Mom, I don't care how much you thought you loved him, why would you marry someone who would deceive your parents and keep you in the dark about your own wedding? Especially someone so mean that he would knock you around?"

"At that time I didn't know he had deceived them. And it suddenly all seemed very romantic to me. Like my knight in shining armor who chose me out of all the young maidens in the village and loved me so much that he'd surprise me this way and whisk me off into the sunset on his white horse. Besides, he never appeared mean. He was always mannerly and thoughtful to all of us. I didn't know how he really was. And I'd never seen any of the men in our families beat up their wives and children, so why would I even think that a man would do such a thing? I just figured we'd live happily ever after."

"So, when was the first time he hit you?"

"We'd been married about a month. One day while your dad was gone, I was sweeping the wooden floor in our kitchen, happy to be a wife cleaning her own little place, when I noticed a loose board. With childlike curiosity I lifted the end of it and peered below. It was dark down there, but when my eyes finally adjusted, I saw a number of bottles filled with brown-colored liquid lying in rows on the ground. I was really excited! This was a mystery and I couldn't wait to share it with my new husband.

"As soon as he got home, I took him by the hand and danced him into the kitchen, saying 'I want to show you something.' I knelt over and eagerly pulled up the board. 'Look at what I found! What's in those bottles and what do you think they're doing there?'

"Clyde didn't move. Just stared at me. His piercing blue eyes turned cold. Suddenly, he doubled up his fist and knocked me backwards onto the floor. I was horrified and confused. This was the man I loved and who loved me. Why was my knight, who was supposed to protect me, acting this way? My right jaw ached, already puffy. *Something is terribly wrong!* I thought. 'But wha . . .' I started to ask. Before I could get the words out, he hit me again. I started screaming and sobbing and he just hit me harder.

" 'Don't you ever ask me about those bottles again! And don't go telling anyone about them. This will teach you to not go poking your nose into things that are private, that are none of your business! If I want you to know something, I'll tell you.' Then he just walked out the front door and left me there in a huddle, bleeding and crying. As if he didn't even care."

I realized I had been holding my breath, mesmerized by the painful words falling from my mother's lips. I let out a long sad sigh. *What a horrible experience for a new little bride! What a terrible way to learn that your husband is not the person you thought he was. My poor little mommy.* "I'm so sorry," I said, the words catching in my throat as I reached out and pulled her close. Our tears mingled as we clung together.

The lump of pain was so large in my throat that I thought I would gag. Finally, when I could speak, I asked, "Why didn't you leave Dad once you found out what he was like? It would have been easier before we children were born."

Mom wiped the long raven strands of hair from the sides of her face where they had been plastered by tears. Her cameo skin was flawless except for the remnants of a fading bruise on the lower right side of her face. *She is so beautiful! And so gentle. She looks like a queen, the same Queen Esther in the Bible she was named after. No wonder Dad picked her out of all the others.* My heart ached to think of all she had endured. Her large hazel eyes softened as they looked into mine.

"I didn't leave because I loved him. He wasn't mean to me all the time. You know, just like he isn't mean to us all the time now. Quite often he is pleasant, even jokes with us and takes us places. Remember that doll bed and furniture set he hand-carved for you for Christmas when you were little? He worked so hard on it and painted it that perfect shade of blue that you like."

I remember. I loved that set and treasured it for years. Until he smashed it to pieces!

"It's just that we don't know what is going to set him off, nor when. So we live in fear. Back then, he was more loving and did nice things for me, especially after he beat me up. I knew that it was only when I asked him about something that I wasn't supposed to, or did something he didn't like, that he would beat me. At first, I didn't think I deserved his mistreatment, but as time wore on I thought if I would just try harder and be a better wife, he would outgrow what I thought was just a youthful temper."

"Isn't it strange how Dad is always trying to 'teach' somebody something by beating them up?" I interrupted. "I remember the story you told me of how when we lived in Arkansas, Dad hit a man in the head with a pole ax and he almost died. Dad accused him of stealing fish from his trot-line. No wonder the poor man carried a gun for months afterward, once he recovered! I still can't believe that judge only fined Dad $25 for 'disturbing the peace' when he appeared in court. Disturbing the peace, my eye! That man would be dead had the other men not grabbed Dad's arms and held him."

"Yes, your father still brags about how lucky he was that the judge happened to know the other man and had a grudge against him."

No wonder Dad thinks he can get away with anything, even murder.

"For your sake, Mom, I wish you could have left Dad before we kids were born. It's not that I'm sorry I was born. As bad as things are sometimes, I love being alive and am thankful that I exist. There is so much beauty in this world, beauty that you have taught me to appreciate, Mom. I shudder to think of missing out on life."

"You almost did," she said sadly.

"What do you mean?"

"Your dad never really wanted me to have a baby—said he didn't want the responsibility. He beat me up several times hoping I would abort you, but thank God I didn't. After you were born he got to thinking how he'd like a son so when I was pregnant with Chuck he didn't beat me up, hoping for a boy. After Chuck was born he didn't want any more kids so he beat me up every time I got pregnant and caused me to miscarry. But thank God I carried Chris until she was born.

"When Chris was little your dad became very upset when I got pregnant again. When his beatings didn't cause me to miscarry he made an appointment with an out-of-town doctor to do an abortion. But I was so terrified I miscarried in the doctor's office while waiting my turn."

Speechless with shock at all the pain she had gone through, I could only stare in disbelief. To ease the suffocating ache in my throat, I looked away as tears trickled down my face.

"But I really did try to get away from him, honey."

"What do you mean, try?"

"Those bottles that I saw under the kitchen floor were filled with illegal whiskey. Your daddy's mom had set him and his older and younger brothers up in an illegal moonshine business. Oklahoma was a dry state, and their still produced enough corn liquor to supply most of the county, including many in the local sheriff's department. They also supplied the booze for the local bawdy house, which their mom helped run. As you know, their mom supported their family following Clyde's father's mysterious death when he was only three."

I had often wondered about my paternal grandfather's death, but learned early not to ask. Mom had warned us that the price of our curiosity could be very costly. There was a mystery about Dad's side of the family that intrigued me. There seemed to be tons of relatives on my mother's side of the family—so many cousins that I'd not even met them all. But not on my father's side. Dad's family appeared to consist of only his two brothers, their wives and children, and Dad's mom—and her succession of either husbands or live-ins. *Dad has to have other relatives,* I often thought. *But why won't he talk about them?*

As always, when the truth is missing, there is a proliferation of rumors. From one paternal cousin we heard that Dad's grandfather had been hanged as a horse thief. From another, it was rumored that my father had been named after the infamous Clyde Barrow, who was a distant renegade uncle of some sorts.

"So, when did you try to leave Dad? And why couldn't you?"

"I'm getting to that part. My mother found out about the illegal still while I was carrying you. Your dad didn't want to be bothered with me because I was so sick during my pregnancy, so he dumped me on your granny and grandpa. They were thrilled to have me with them, where they knew you and I would be safe, away your father's beatings.

"Clyde did pride himself, however, on being a responsible person when it came to paying his debts. Just as he still does. Just before you were to be born, he paid a local doctor in advance to deliver you. He then left on a hunting trip feeling pretty good about himself. We learned later that the doctor's medical license had been revoked for drunken malpractice. Since Clyde had paid him in a case of moonshine, the 'doctor' showed up drunk. Your granny assisted him, but when he started to yank your umbilical cord out instead of cutting it, she pushed him aside and forced him to leave. Grabbing some scissors, she cut the cord herself and finished taking care of both of us. Had she not taken over, who knows what might have happened.

"Immediately after you were born, your granny called the revenuers, who came and destroyed the still. Your dad and his older brother were sent to prison for a year, but their youngest brother didn't have to go since he was so young.

"You and I stayed at home with my folks while your father was in prison. I was worried sick, but thank goodness nobody ever learned your granny was the one who called the Feds. I decided that I was going to leave your father after he got out of prison. When he finally showed up, I was scared to death, but I told him I wanted a divorce."

My pulse quickened as I imagined the scene. "What did Dad say?"

"Nothing. He was quiet for a minute and just grinned that grin of his. 'That's okay, honey,' he finally said with a sneer. 'You can have a divorce, but I'm keeping the baby.'

"I was surprised and wondered why he now suddenly wanted the responsibility of a baby, especially since I knew he liked the ladies. But when I objected, he just laughed and said, 'I have friends in the sheriff's department who owe me favors. They'll swear that you are an unfit mother, that you slept with them all the time I was gone, and believe me, I *will* get the baby. So go ahead and divorce me if you want to.' Then he leaned back and laughed."

I can just see him! I didn't think I could hate him any more, but now I do! I thought. My anger quickly turned into guilt, however. *Oh, my! It was Mom's love for me, her baby, that held her as Dad's captive. Had it not been for* me *she would be free. I've got to do something to help! But what?*

My mind raced toward the thoughts I had been entertaining for weeks. Now they were doubly fueled. *Dad is not going to keep on winning! The next time he starts beating Mom and threatening us with his gun, I will somehow get it and shoot him! So help me, God!*

Chapter Three

The Bitter Fruits of Frustration

The pressure swelled within me. I knew what I had to do—but shoot my own father? Could I really do that? *I've got to look for another way out.* For several months I considered various options.

I could try to convince our mother to take us children and leave. That was a most unlikely option. We knew that if we fled to sympathetic relatives for refuge, our father would find us, and their lives as well as ours would be endangered.

I could call the police and have my father arrested. From experience, I knew that option would be an exercise in futility. When I was eleven years old, I had snuck to a neighbor's house one night and called the police but our terrified mother refused to press charges. Even if she had, they couldn't keep him in jail forever.

I could run away from home. I could just leave, but I feared that my newfound freedom might lead to a worse prison. I had heard horrible stories about runaways. I feared I might become another child of the street—one of the many who are sucked into oblivion through crime, addiction, or prostitution, since I wouldn't be able to adequately support myself. And yet, didn't I deserve a chance at life? What hope did I have at home? Nothing there was going to change, except get worse. If I left, I might be a lucky runaway.

I could marry as early as possible. I seriously considered this, but seeing firsthand the negative results of a teen marriage, I did not want to repeat my mother's mistake. Because Mom married when she was fourteen and I was born when she was fifteen, she was forced to stay in her abusive marriage. If I followed in her footsteps, I would be destined to repeat history and the cycle of abuse would likely continue. But didn't I deserve a chance for happiness? Maybe a better candidate than my dad would come along and my marriage might be a good one.

I could remain at home. My home situation would not likely improve, but by staying, I could at least give my siblings and mother my love and moral support. I also would not expose myself to worse unknown dangers. While providing no quick fix for my pain, this choice might be my best, considering my list of poor options. But to stay home and remain miserable seemed unthinkable.

I could eliminate the source of my problem. From time to time I heard or read about individuals who were acquitted for shooting someone in self-defense. *Maybe I wouldn't be convicted either,* I thought. *Surely the courts would understand that I was only defending my family.* But what if I were convicted? I feared I couldn't handle prison. And yet, wasn't there a chance I might be acquitted?

I could commit suicide. I was a likely candidate. Not only was I unhappy and afraid, I was tired of my heavy burden of responsibility. And those recurring dreams of helplessness were getting worse. I fought frequent bouts of depression and carried the added weight of low self-esteem. I was a failure. It was obvious I couldn't protect or rescue my mom and siblings. And if we were to somehow escape from Dad, how would I provide for them? I believed my father when he told me I was ugly and stupid and that I would never amount to anything. If I was so worthless that even my own father recognized it, what hope did I have for a happy future? Life just didn't seem to offer much.

Which option should I choose? Did I really have a choice or was I just a pawn in the game of life?

A CHOICE IS MADE

One day I read a newspaper article that reported the acquittal of a teenage boy who had shot and killed his father during an attack upon the mother.

Good for him! I thought. *That father got exactly what he deserved.* I laid the paper down, but I couldn't get the article out of my mind. *Surely a jury wouldn't convict me, either, for defending my family if I shot my father. But even if it did, so what? At least Mom and the kids would be free.*

But each time I imagined how I might grab the gun from him, I was plagued by fears. *What if during his next attack I can't get the gun? If I were able to wrestle it from him, could I really force myself to take aim at him and deliberately pull the trigger? What if I attempted and failed? He'll kill us all!*

But my greatest fear was that I might succeed.

I was so tenderhearted, it pained me to see a dead mouse in a trap. I rescued countless injured birds that had fallen from their nests and took them to the loving hands of my mother who, after nursing them to health, set them free. For years I grieved after Dad's sleep was disturbed one night by the whining of our dog's puppies; he brutally killed them. Following a search the next morning, I stumbled upon their bloody bodies strewn among the weeds.

What is the matter with me? It hurts me to see a dead animal; how can I even think of killing my own father, no matter how terrible he is? But I am my family's only hope, I argued. *If I don't do something, who will?*

One night my heart cried out to a God I had heard about from Granny—but I wasn't even sure he actually existed. Granny seemed to have a lot of faith in Him and I was desperate. *God, if You're as powerful as Granny says,* I prayed, *then why don't You do something? Why doYou allow my dad to be so mean to us?*

From the depths of my anguished soul I pleaded, *If You really do exist, please help me. I didn't ask to be born into this situation. I'm supposed to do something, but I don't know what. When Chuck and Chris are terrified as Mom is being beaten, I try to keep them quiet so Dad won't get more upset. I tell them that everything will be okay, but I know it won't. After Dad leaves and slams the door, I hold Mom close and tell her how sorry I am that she is hurt. I can't fix this problem, God. It's too big and I'm too small. But if You won't do something, I guess I'll have to.*

I wept bitter tears into my pillow and decided, *God's not real, anyway. How could He care?*

At an age when most teenagers look forward to a happy future with joyful anticipation, I waited for my dad's next attack—the perfect provocation for me to shoot him.

A NEW DIRECTION

One Sunday afternoon shortly after my prayer, my Uncle Paul stopped by and asked, "Kitty, would you like to go to church with us this evening?"

"Dad says religion is a crutch for weaklings, so I don't think he'll let me," I answered. "But I'd like to."

"Why don't you ask him? He might."

For some strange reason, I found myself really wanting to go, pleading silently as I went to ask permission. *God, if religion is just a crutch then I must qualify, because I feel like I'm falling apart. I really need something to lean on.*

Surprisingly, Dad let me go.

I sat spellbound by the message I heard that night. The minister spoke of how each of us lives under the penalty of death. He said that we are hopelessly and helplessly trapped as prisoners in a world that is terminally polluted with sin—sin that resulted from Adam and Eve's wrong choice in the Garden of Eden. He then spoke of a loving God who provided a way for us to escape—a way that offered freedom instead of bondage, victory instead of defeat, and love instead of hate.

I longed for freedom and how I craved the love of a father! *But how could God love me?* I wondered. *I don't deserve any of these good things since I am so worthless. My earthly father doesn't love me, how can I expect a perfect God to love me? Especially since I have these evil thoughts in my heart.*

But the speaker stressed the heavenly Father's love, His goodness, and how He could be trusted to keep His word. He held up his tattered black Bible and read from it John 3:16—"For God so loved the world that he gave his only Son, so that everyone who believes in him will not perish but have eternal life."

As he spoke, a strange thing happened. He suddenly stopped and, pointing his finger it seemed as though straight at me, declared in a loud voice, "And 'whosoever' has to include you, because God is not a liar!"

I was stunned. *It must be true,* I reasoned. *A God this loving wouldn't deliberately leave someone out, so His invitation has to include me!*

The best part was it didn't matter that I didn't deserve it, for the minister went on to explain that God's love and forgiveness is a gift. Through Christ, His Son, God was offering love, not judgment; forgiveness, not condemnation. He offered life because He had conquered death through the cross and resurrection. I didn't understand all that I heard, but a tiny spark of hope began to glimmer.

I had no time to go on a worldwide theological search for spiritual truths. Time was running out. I had to make a decision. *I can choose to pursue the path to kill my father,* I thought, *or I can choose the door opening before me and trust God with my life.*

As I weighed my choices, the minister explained that to accept God, I had to interact with Him in a personal way. "You don't just try to keep a set of rules in hopes of impressing God into loving you; God already loves you."

Then he added, "All of the great religions of the world tell us that we should to try to reach God by living good and honest lives, loving our enemies, and forgiving those who wrong us. Their books tell us what we should do, but they don't tell us *how* to do it. They just give us more rules.

"Christianity, based on the Holy Bible, is different," he explained. "It's not a religion—though sadly some Christians treat it like it is—by just counting how many times they go to church and how much money they give. But that's just like keeping more rules. Becoming a Christian is all about having a relationship with the one and only living God. A God who doesn't ask us to try to reach Him through our own feeble efforts—He knows we can't. It is through Christ that God reaches down to us on our level, right where we are, regardless of our condition, and invites us to Him.

"You see," he went on, "we are changed after we accept Christ, for it is only then that we have the power to become all that God created us to be. Not before."

My mind raced with excitement. *If I don't have to clean up my act in order to be accepted by God, then maybe there is a chance for me. This is my only hope!* I decided, bowing my head. From the depths of my soul came the admission, *I need You, God. I want You in my life. It's hard for me to believe that all of these things could be true, but I don't have anywhere else to go. Please forgive me and help me to become what You want me to be.*

It was actually more of a pleading than anything, for I could not put into words the needs of my soul. But it didn't matter. God, who hears the faintest cry of the weakest heart, heard mine and answered its longings. Very softly and gently His love entered my heart and life, and a miracle took place. The heavy burden that I had carried was lifted and, for the first time in my life, I was free.

Little did I know how much the choice I made that evening would impact my entire life. But this choice did not come with a free pass from pain. And the pain I had experienced before was nothing compared to what lay ahead!

SO WHERE ARE THE ROSES?

God never promised us a rose garden. He did promise us, however, strength and power to function within a bitter and thorny environment.

> Sometimes, God doesn't change our circumstances, He changes us in our circumstances.
>
> —Carla Killough McClafferty, *Forgiving God*

I returned home that night to the same circumstances, the same danger, and the same heartaches. Nothing there had changed. But I had. Through Christ I was a new person, a child of God, whom He had promised to love and strengthen. I didn't know then how much I would need God's love and strength, for the situation at home not only didn't improve, it worsened. But for the moment I had a breather. A lull before the storm.

Dad allowed me to attend church only a few times after that, but I prayed and studied the Bible the pastor gave me. I grew stronger, and my attitude began to change, but I needed to be with other Christians. There was so much in the Bible I didn't understand. I had so many questions but there was no one to ask. Granny could have answered them, but she lived too far away. Uncle Paul moved out of town, and I had no way to attend church, even if Dad had let me.

Lord, I really need to go to church. I'm getting depressed again, and I feel like I'm fighting a losing battle with my flare-ups of hate.

When I was sixteen, some young people invited me to their church and, to my surprise, Dad let me attend. I joined the church and was baptized. Although I still couldn't attend as often as I wanted, I was allowed to go on Sunday mornings. I began to blossom spiritually as I was nurtured in the loving atmosphere of the church and fellow Christians.

I found the more I responded to God's Word and strove to live by it, the stronger I grew. Anger still flared, as was natural, especially during Dad's brutal outbursts, but it didn't consume me.

Though my father's episodes seemed to be lessening in frequency, I noticed a new subtlety on his part. After beating my mother, he would often verbalize his reasons. "Your mother nags me too much." "I've had a bad day." Or, "It's because you kids upset me." There was always some excuse.

What's with his excuses? I wondered. I suspected he longed for the younger ones' affection and didn't want them to be afraid of him. He probably felt it was too late to fool me, for I had seen too much of his brutality, but he might be able to convince Chuck and Chris that he wasn't responsible for his actions.

Something else bothered me. His violent episodes appeared to coincide with the times I was gone, and this became an added burden for me. As a teenager I needed outside activities, but because I felt responsible for the family's safety, I worried all the time I was gone. This new perception led me to unexpected bursts of hate and resentment that I feared would destroy me. Many nights I fell into a fitful sleep, praying, "Lord, I know I'm supposed to pray for my enemies, but it's hard when the enemy is my own father."

One night just before graduation, I returned home from a church service to find Dad beating Mom with his gun. I remember it clearly—it was a Colt 45 on a 38 frame. *Oh, no, Lord! What triggered him this time?* I ran to Mother's side and pushed myself between them.

Suddenly I felt the cold steel muzzle of his gun jam hard into my temple. My heart raced, pounding wildly against the Bible I clutched close to my chest.

"One of these days I'm going to blow your head off. I'm sick and tired of your interfering," my father said evenly, without emotion. His steel blue eyes bored into mine.

Suddenly, an inner voice from deep within me said, *Now is your chance. Why don't you just wrestle the gun from his hand and shoot him? He isn't getting any better, he's only getting worse. Things will never change. Just grab the gun and get it over with.*

I stood still, barely breathing. The thoughts continued, seductive in their rationale. *Surely God would understand. After all, how much does He expect you to endure? Why don't you just do what you planned to do years ago?*

Suddenly, I recalled some words I had recently read: "Don't be afraid of those who want to kill you. They can only kill your body; they cannot touch your soul. Fear only God, who can destroy both your soul and your body in hell" (Matthew 10:28), and "Don't be afraid, for I am with you. Do not be dismayed, for I am your God. I will strengthen you. I will help you. I will uphold you with my victorious right hand" (Isaiah 41:10).

The tempter's voice sneered, *Yeah, just like He's helping you right now, with a gun pointed to your head! That's helping?*

Another Scripture sprang to mind: " 'For I know the plans I have for you,' says the LORD. 'They are plans for good and not for disaster, to give you a future and a hope' " (Jeremiah 29:11). *Please help me, Lord! I want to believe Your words and trust this situation to You!*

Staring unflinchingly into the eyes of my father, I said softly, "If that's what you want to do,

Dad, go ahead and pull the trigger. I'm ready to die. I'll just go to heaven and be where you can't hurt me anymore. But remember this, some day you will stand before God and be held accountable for your actions." I said this firmly, but with respect.

He saw no fear in my eyes, but for the first time I saw a glimmer of what looked like fear in his. He lowered the gun and never again threatened me in that way.

~

On graduation night I numbly walked across the stage and accepted my diploma. For years, Mom had looked forward to my high school graduation ceremony, but my dad had beaten her so badly she couldn't attend. Chuck, my only family supporter in attendance, gave me a hug before we quickly left. I couldn't bear to stay and watch the happy families around me.

But even worse pain was yet to come.

Chapter Four

The Escape

The fall following my high school graduation, I began my first full-time job as a secretary in an elementary school near our home. I loved the students and adored the principal, a petite, dynamic woman just under five feet tall. Mrs. Watts commanded loving respect from everyone, even children taller than she.

That first year was wonderful. Though we continued to tiptoe around our volcano at home, there weren't too many violent eruptions. I began dating the local junior high football coach and life was good—as good as it could be. But not for long.

Very early one morning, several days before my nineteenth birthday, Dad began beating Mother and I intervened. Pushing myself between him and Mom, I asked softly, "Dad, if you are so miserable with us, why don't you just leave?"

"No one will ever make me leave my house," he snarled. "You leave," and he punched me in the face. Mom lunged for the phone. For the first time she called the police. After knocking me to the floor, Dad tried to wrestle the phone from her, but not before her screams for the police were heard by the operator.

A LINE IS DRAWN

This time Mother planned to press charges. She had drawn a line in the sand, regardless of the consequences, for life or death; we could no longer live this way.

The officers came, handcuffed Dad, and took him to jail. Our hearts pounded as we rushed to the courthouse. We had been instructed to be there at 8:30 a.m. if we wanted to press formal charges. *Maybe this is the beginning of our freedom,* I hoped. But hope turned to horror when we arrived shortly after 8:00 and learned that Dad had been released. The one who had threatened to kill us if we ever reported him now waited at home for us.

My heart raced and my palms were sticky. I opened my mouth, but there was nothing I could say in response to the clerk. I whirled around, facing Mom and the children. Mom's shoulders suddenly sagged. Her eyes, wide in terror, stared at me like a frightened fawn as her face crumpled. Chris began sobbing silently as she buried her face into Mom's arm, clinging to her. Chuck's pale face showed no emotion, but his fists were doubled at his sides.

My mind, foggy with fear, went blank. What could I do for our little family? The line that Mom had so courageously drawn was now full circle and we were trapped within it. *Lord, what can we do?*

We couldn't go to neighbors. We couldn't go to Granny's house—it was hours away. Besides, that was one of the first places he would look. There was no way out. We were doomed.

Suddenly the fog cleared. *The church! That's the only safe place.*

I herded everyone into the car and then quickly drove to the church. Dr. Hope, our pastor, sat stunned as we explained our situation. He listened to us and prayed with us. He never left our side. He drove us to the courthouse, where we filed assault and battery charges against Dad. He recommended an attorney and then drove us to his office, where Mom filed for a divorce. We stayed at the church most of that day where we felt safe and secure.

Mom called a next-door neighbor and apprised her of the situation. "I saw the police car," Mrs. Shaw said, "when they brought your dad back to the house. Then later, I saw the police car return and take Clyde away again in handcuffs."

We breathed easier and felt it was safe for us to return home. At least for a while.

Dad had time to think in jail, and to assess his situation. He was in a tough spot. His private treatment of us was now on public record. He knew that Mother would have no problem getting a divorce. She would likely be awarded the house along with monthly child support. His plan to use temporary insanity as a plea for killing us was less plausible than ever.

Three months prior to this, Mom had made her decision to accept Christ as her personal Savior and had been baptized. Dad had noticed a change in her, just as he had noticed the change in me following my spiritual choice years earlier.

Now it was his turn to make a spiritual decision. But there was one major difference: Behind his "choice" lay an ulterior motive. He most likely recalled a statement Mom had made that if ever they were separated, the only way they could get back together was if he were a new person spiritually.

Dad called Dr. Hope and asked him and some of the church deacons to come and pray with him, saying he wanted to become a Christian. They went, talked with him, prayed with him, and read Scriptures. After a long discussion, Dad prayed a wonderful "prayer of repentance."

As a result of his "conversion," we dropped all charges and Dad returned home. He went before the church, gave a splashy testimony as to how he had been changed by God, and this charismatic new convert was baptized. The church rejoiced, for a sinner had come home.

And indeed he had! Two weeks later he was beating Mom again. We were more miserable than ever, for we knew we'd been conned—and so had the church. But they didn't know it. Yet.

During an Independence Day family outing at a public park, while my parents were on a walk, my dad again attacked our mother. We heard her screams. We ran toward her as she stumbled out of a wooded section, blood streaming down her face. She gasped out her story of how Dad had become angry and beaten her on the side of the head with a rock. People gathered around, staring helplessly, as I tried to wipe the blood from Mom's face. Dad quickly strode into view.

He smiled warmly at everyone and stated calmly, "She is hysterical, poor thing. Fell and hit her head on a rock." Relief spread across the faces of some of the men nearest us when Dad lifted Mom up by the waist and said gently, “Here, sweetheart, it’s okay.” Believing my father’s story relieved the onlookers of any responsibility in this situation. But we children knew the truth, and it wasn’t okay.

A sense of urgency pounded within me. *We have to get away from him soon, but how?*

Several days later, Mom asked Dad if she could take us children and go to visit her sister in San Francisco for a few weeks to recuperate. Dad was quiet for a moment, mentally chewing on the idea. Finally he agreed, but said we children had to remain. Mom blanched and looked out the window, brows knitted in deep concentration. I thought she was going to change her mind, but she said, “Okay.”

Our home wasn’t the same without our good-natured and cheery mother, but we were relieved that she was safe away from Dad. For the moment. We didn’t know of her plans to stay longer than she had told our dad, nor that she was forming a plan of escape.

One evening the phone rang and Dad answered. He talked for a while, then hung up and announced, “That was your mom. She has decided to stay in California. Says she doesn’t love you kids anymore and wants to get on with her life.”

Chris began to cry and Chuck’s face crumpled.

I whispered as Dad left the room, “Don’t believe a word of what he says—Mother does love us. She would never leave us.”

We learned later that Dad had often called Mom, telling her to stay in California, stating we children didn’t love her, that we would be happier without her, and that if she knew what was good for her she wouldn’t return home.

THE DECISION: GO OR STAY?

A week later, I began my second year as school secretary. There was much to do to prepare for the onslaught of excited school children, but Mrs. Watts and I somehow accomplished it.

Early in the morning, one day before school was to start, the school phone rang. It was my mother. Thinking she was still in California, I said excitedly, “Hi, Mom!” But something was strange. She was whispering.

“Kitty, I’m home. Your Aunt Martha and Cousin Abner drove me here and will help us go back to California. This is our only chance to get away from your dad. Check Chris out of her classroom there, drive to Chuck’s school, check him out, and come home immediately. I’m already packing.”

Stunned, I cradled the phone in its stand. Mrs. Watts stared at my pale face. “What’s wrong?" Even as I explained to her what was happening, I struggled within. Mrs. Watts was one of the few people who knew about my home situation. She was also one of the few who knew the real cause of the bruises that sometimes appeared on my face. She often hugged me, saying, "I love you like my own daughter."

Suddenly, I stood at a crossroads that required another important choice. Should I leave or stay? I had grown very fond of Jim, the coach I was dating. There were definite romantic possibilities. He was a strong but gentle young man who cared for me deeply. I felt secure with him. I loved Mrs. Watts and I loved my job, especially the children there. How could I leave them all so abruptly, without warning or explanation?

But how would Mom, Chuck, and Chris make it without me? They couldn't support themselves. Mom, with only a fourth-grade education, didn't even know how to drive. Dad would surely find them, and I wouldn't be there to protect them.

If I stayed, I knew Dad would find me. Not only would my life be in danger but also the lives of anyone who helped me. What was I to do? Fierce pain pierced my heart as it was yanked in opposite directions. Suddenly, I was aware of someone calling my name.

"Kitty, listen to me. Please don't go. You're too young to have such a responsibility. You can stay with me. Besides, you can't help them anymore. Maybe your father will see that it's all over once they're in California and he won't follow them. He'll just give up."

Love glowed in her tear-filled eyes as Mrs. Watts took me by the shoulders and shook me gently. "You deserve a chance to be happy, so stay and live your own life. We'll get legal help to see that your father doesn't bother you. Don't go."

Lord, I pleaded inwardly, *please help me. I don't know what to do. I don't have time to reason out all the advantages and disadvantages of my options.*

The room wasn't cold, but I started shaking. Somewhere in the deep recesses of my storm-tossed mind, icy winds of confusion whirled in darkness, chilling me to the core. I stood there, frozen in the cold reality of my emotional turbulence. From somewhere, a soft light formed a tiny spot deep within the center of my soul—a warm, calm, and quiet spot that seemed to pulsate as it enlarged. Its center revealed the choice I must make.

"I'm so sorry, Mrs. Watts," I stammered. "I must go. Please forgive me for leaving you at a time when you need me the most. How will you find a replacement on such short notice? And then there's Jim. It will break his heart that I left without saying goodbye. Would you please explain everything to him? I can't let anyone know where we are going. Not even you. We can't let my father find us!"

She lifted her head, and holding it high in determination she said, "Don't worry, I will take care of everything." Her breath caught as she gave me a long, hard hug and said, "I understand why you have to do what you are doing. I love you. You will be in my prayers constantly."

Heart pounding, I gathered up Chris and Chuck and rushed home.

Everything was in chaos there. Mother and Aunt Martha were tossing things into bags while Cousin Abner pushed items into the trunk of my aunt's car.

Comprehension of the scene around me paralyzed me with fear. *What if Dad catches us as we are trying to leave?* I glanced fearfully at the driveway. *Why can't I think clearly? How do I choose what to take from all of my possessions when space is so limited?*

"Kitty, grab your things and put them into these pillowcases," Mom commanded, tossing them to me. "They will pack easier. Put them in our car trunk; your aunt's is almost full." After poking as much as we could into every available space, we jumped into the two cars and sped off, pursued only by our terror.

"Head for Granny's house," Mom said. "We've got to take her with us. That's the first place your dad will look, and she'll be in danger." Grandpa had died years earlier from cancer and Granny had remarried. Mom felt Dad was no threat to our step-grandpa.

After the three-hour trip to Hatfield, Arkansas, we picked up Granny and headed straight for California. Fear pushed us farther and faster with every mile. I looked in the rear-view mirror constantly, expecting to see my dad barreling down upon us. Other than for gas and quick pit stops and bites to eat, we fled nonstop to Needles, California, where we collapsed in a motel.

UNCLE JOHN'S HOUSE

The next morning we drove to Delhi, California, to my great uncle John's tiny house, where we were welcomed with open and loving arms. We had never met Uncle John, but we quickly fell in love with this man whose heart was twice as big as the meager abode he lovingly shared with us. We thanked God that he wholeheartedly sheltered our bedraggled, frightened family, quite possibly at the risk of his own life. Though we slept on pallets and our quarters were cramped, we were happy because we were free. At least for a while.

Uncle John was Granny's oldest brother, a widower with an irresistible sense of humor.

"Honey," he said, holding up a can of beans our first evening there, "don't ever eat pork and beans."

"Why not?" I asked, wide-eyed.

"Because you'll go blind."

"Why would eating pork and beans cause me to go blind?" I asked, walking perfectly into his trap.

"Because," he answered, eyes twinkling, "you'll go blind looking for the pork."

He then showed us two square little boards, which he described as ant killers. "How on earth can those little boards kill ants?" I asked.

"I'll show you," he said, picking up a board. "You take an ant, place him on this here board like this. Then you take the other board and whack him real hard. Kills the ant every time."

He cooked cornbread in a big iron skillet, serving up thick slices with glasses of cold milk. We felt right at home.

~

I put in applications everywhere for secretarial work, and we did whatever we could to help put food on the table. We picked up walnuts and harvested grapes in the local vineyards. For a time I worked at an almond-processing plant. Three elderly ladies and I sat in front of two conveyor belts where we sorted the almond nutmeats from the shells coming toward us on one belt and tossed them onto the other belt. I sat at the head of the assembly line and was the first one for the cracked almonds to reach. The women were pleasant and I enjoyed their light-hearted conversation. I was quick and worked hard, but soon the job became boring. My only challenge was to see how fast I could work.

"Child, you should slow down a little. You're working too hard," the lady next to me cautioned. The other two ladies chimed in and agreed.

I replied, with a quick toss of my long blond hair, "Oh, I don't mind," and reached in front of her for a missed nutmeat. "I like working hard. It makes the time go by faster."

Then the foreman cautioned me to slow down. "You don't have to work so hard, Kitty. There are three other ladies." Pleased by all of this kind attention, I only worked faster.

"I can't believe how nice everyone is there," I announced to everyone during supper one evening. "They actually worry about me working too hard!"

Thus, I was devastated when I received a "pink slip" with my next paycheck. Fighting back tears, I stammered "But why? I've been a hard worker." *Besides, I really need this job!* I screamed inside. The foreman just shrugged and thanked me for the time I had worked there. Later, I put the clues together and figured out why.

The other ladies had worked there faithfully for years, and they must have felt threatened, besides being bored. I did the work of several people, which left little for them to do. Despite all of their strong hints, I had refused to slow down. The foreman knew that with my youthful energy and ambition, I would leave this minimum wage job for a better-paying one as soon as I could (and he was right). He must have concluded that it was wiser to let one worker go now than to later look for four new ones.

OUR SHORT-LIVED HAVEN

Meanwhile, back in Texas, Dad had sweet-talked an elderly neighbor into telling him she had noted California license plates on one of the cars we left in. Dad assumed we had fled to the town of Taft, where my mom's youngest brother Paul lived. This was the same uncle who had taken me to church that eventful night years earlier where I made the choice that changed my life's journey forever.

Dad sent mail to Mom via Uncle Paul, knowing it would be forwarded. At first, Dad tried threats. "If you know what's good for you, you'll get back here with Chuck and Chris. I'm getting tired of this nonsense," his letters warned.

When he received no response after sending a number of letters, he changed his tactics. He tried appealing to mother's soft side. "I really need my sweet little wife and children. I miss you so much...I am terribly lonely." Mom continued to ignore his letters.

I found work at the *Turlock Daily Journal*, a few miles away, as a proofreader. Mom, who sewed beautifully, applied for a position as housekeeper and seamstress for a Turlock physician and family. After interviewing her, Dr. and Mrs. Collins introduced her to their children, who liked her immediately. She was hired, but they wanted personal references. Mom gave them the names and addresses of close friends back in Texas whom we trusted. At the top of the list was our pastor's name. "If we can't trust our pastor, who can we trust?" Mom commented as she folded the list and put it into an envelope for her new employer. I agreed. But we were both wrong.

Dad was furious because Mom had gotten away from him despite his threats. He was even angrier because she refused to return. He had lost control of her, and that was unforgivable.

We had no way of knowing it at that time, but Dad really had a heyday at church after we "abandoned" him. Our sudden departure had provided the perfect springboard for his lies. Dad wept bitter tears before the new pastor, Chad Termilian. (Dr. Hope had retired and Pastor Termilian had moved into his position.) Dad told everyone at church who would listen about his mistreatment by a deranged wife who had poisoned the minds of his precious children against him—a wife whom he still loved with all of his heart and wanted back despite her wrong actions. Though he had tried to be a perfect father, he said, especially after becoming a Christian, he must have somehow failed God.

Dad was very convincing. After receiving a reference request from Dr. Collins, Pastor Termilian wrote back that mother was so mentally and emotionally incompetent that he could not recommend her for employment. Fortunately, Mom had already established credibility with the Collins' family who found her to be an efficient, responsible, and gentle woman of integrity. They simply did not believe the pastor and gave his letter to Mom.

We were shocked, heartbroken, and confused by our former assistant pastor's response.

"Why would Pastor Termilian say something so terrible, Mom?" I cried.

Mother, more angry than tearful, said through clenched teeth, "I suspect Clyde got to him with his conning personality."

"But he knew us just as well as Dr. Hope did. I was president of the Young Women's Auxiliary for a whole year. I was a leader in Sunday school, I sang in the choir, as did you shortly after you joined the church, long before Dad's sudden jailhouse conversion. He knew how Dr. Hope hid us out at the church most of that day when Dad was put in jail. He knew our entire situation." I stood there, shaking my head in puzzlement, tears ready to spill.

"I know," Mother said sadly and walked away. His stab of betrayal plunged deep into her heart, as it did mine.

We had no way of knowing that Dad was experiencing anything other than anger from a wounded ego of a rejected husband and father who was trying to gain sympathy from the friends of his rebellious wife. Only much later did we realize he was laying the foundation for a diabolical plan. And what better people could he have in his corner than kind and trusting God-fearing people?

~

Shortly afterwards, we excitedly moved into an inexpensive apartment near downtown Turlock. Granny had already returned to her home in Arkansas.

Dad began another barrage of letters, again changing his tactics. "I'm very ill. My ulcers are acting up again, but the doctors aren't sure exactly what's wrong...I'm terribly sick...might even die."

"Good!" Mom said, "I hope he does!"

Determined to obtain a response from Mother, Dad sought yet another direction and aimed straight at the most vulnerable part of her heart: the spiritual spot. Mom, not yet developed in spiritual wisdom and discernment, was quickly impressed by anything that smacked of spirituality. Thus, Dad hit the bull's-eye when after several weeks of silence, he wrote that he had "really gotten religion" and was "really changed."

And yet, who of the wisest and most mature Christians wouldn't be impressed by sentences such as, "I will regret for the rest of my life all the pain I have caused you and the children. I don't blame you for not believing me since I betrayed you with my lies before—when I said I was a new person spiritually but I wasn't. I admit it. I lied because I didn't want to face jail another day. And I'm sorry about the letter from the pastor. I think he just misunderstood some of the things I said, but I'll clear it up. Honey, I really am changed. You see, this is what it has taken for God to get my attention.

"Just think about it, I have no reason to lie now. I've already lost the most precious things on earth to me. I know you and the kids won't come back to me, because you don't believe me.

And I don't blame you. I wouldn't believe me, either! I deserve my misery, but you and the kids don't deserve to be miserable—struggling all alone out there—you being so frail and having to work so hard. You deserve better."

Fatigued and weary from overwork and financial struggles, Mom finally succumbed to his persuasion, and gave him our address and phone number. Dad called often and finally Mom agreed to take the children and return to Texas with him during his upcoming Christmas vacation.

"Mom, please don't go back," I begged. "I'm not convinced that he has changed."

"How can you say that? Where is your faith? Don't you trust God anymore?" she asked, shaking her head in disappointment. As do many of us, Mom had difficulty assessing the fine line between faith and presumption.

"Yes. Of course, I still trust God," I said emphatically. "It's Dad I don't trust."

"You can't see into his heart. You're not God."

"That's true, Mom. But God does give us common sense. He tells us to be cautious in our dealings with others, to be wary." Then I quoted a verse from Jesus' own words: "Look, I am sending you out as sheep among wolves. Be wary as snakes and harmless as doves" (Matthew 10:16).

"But, honey, you read his letters. And you talked to him on the phone just like I did. He apologized to you too. Didn't he say he wanted to spend the rest of his life making it up to me and you kids for all the pain he had caused us? Didn't he say he wanted you to go on to college and not have to worry about anybody but yourself for a change? That's the main reason he said he didn't want you to come back with us—so you could get on with your life." Her eyes pleaded for understanding. "Don't those words evidence a changed heart?"

"I'll admit that Dad's words sound good, Mom," I said with a sigh, "but that's all they are—words. His words alone aren't evidence of anything, other than verbal attempts to get you to do what he wants, which is to go back to him. Remember the last time we trusted his words?"

"But he's never sounded like this before. He's obviously a broken and miserable man."

"I know, Mom," I sympathized, patting her shoulder. "Since we can't see the motive behind a person's words, it is difficult to know when someone is telling the truth. But isn't that all the more reason we need to exercise caution? If we are rushed by words, don't we run the risk of making another wrong choice?"

Despite my strong arguments with Mom, I began to experience my own doubts.

Why should I doubt Dad's spiritual change? I know that there is no one beyond the reach of God's love. No one can do anything so bad that God won't hear an honest prayer from that person and change him. Didn't I myself make a dramatic about-face? Didn't I choose a spiritual course that turned me around completely? While struggling with the idea of shooting my own father, I deliberately made the choice to ask Christ into my life and to help me become the kind of person God created me to be. Why is it so unthinkable that Dad could also make that choice?

Despite my inner arguments, a knot grew in the pit of my stomach. *I just wish Mom wouldn't rush into this.*

But it was no use; her mind was made up. Was it because she actually believed Dad's promises, or was it because she wanted or needed to believe them? I'd heard her crying softly at night, and I marveled at this tiny bundle of strength—a little more than 100 pounds of it—and the courage she had shown. She constantly fought emotional fatigue and exhaustion, but she tried to present a cheerful attitude for us children. I knew she worried about me and my future. She voiced no hope for my attending college as long as I was burdened with financial responsibilities for my family.

She also worried about Chuck, in his teens, and Chris, now eleven. They needed a father and a stable home life with adequate food and clothing. Despite his abuse, Dad had always been a hard worker and a good provider. If he were really changed, would she not be morally wrong to stay away from him and subject her children to further deprivation? Sadly, our choices are too often made based upon our wants and our needs rather than upon wisdom.

I, too, wanted to believe Dad. It would be a relief for me if he *were* changed. Then Mom could take the children back to their home, their roots, and their childhood friends without fear. I could return to work, save my money, and start college the following fall. I could finally pursue my personal dreams.

But deep in my heart, I was bothered by a heavy and familiar sense of foreboding. One that I recognized only too well. One that was always right.

Chapter Five

The Fateful Decision

A heavy pall lay over Christmas at our little apartment. The spindly tree, tilting to one side in its stand in the corner, appeared gloomy despite its bright array of ornaments. Dad arrived on December 21, appearing genuinely happy to see us.

Maybe he has changed, I thought. I forced myself to be cheerful, especially for the children, who appeared withdrawn and depressed. Chuck had turned fifteen that fall. Although Dad had promised to buy him a car upon their return, Chuck didn't appear excited.

On December 26, as we stood by the loaded trailer, an icy-chilling loneliness crept over me. I gave Dad a perfunctory hug before he went to the car. I turned to little Chris, who clung to me as Chuck shyly waited his turn beside her.

"I don't want to go back, I'm afraid," Chris whispered through quivering lips.

"I know, sweetheart. But Mom needs you to be strong. Just remember, I will be praying for you." I brushed a long blond strand from the side of her face where it was pasted by tears and kissed her goodbye. She turned slowly and trudged toward the car.

Hearing his sister's whisper, Chuck said brusquely, "Me too," as he hugged me long and hard. He wiped at his eyes and quickly turned away. I wanted to be strong for them, but I couldn't keep my tears hidden. They were going back to a terrifying place, and I was staying behind.

Saying goodbye to Mom was the hardest. She wasn't just my mother, she was my dearest and closest friend on earth. A cheery, witty lifter of my spirits—my confidante and my buddy, who often waited up until I returned home from a date to re-live the evening with me over hot chocolate and laughter. Hugging her frail body close to me, I never felt more protective, nor more helpless.

"I will miss you so much," she said, between soft sobs. "Write often."

"I'll be praying for you day and night, Mom. And you know I'll write." I took a deep breath to hold my own emotions at bay. Mustering a feeble smile, I said, "Don't worry, Mom, everything will be okay."

Never did those words sound so empty, nor could they be more untrue.

As I watched the blue and white Ford disappear from sight, my heart twisted with that old feeling of dread. Had this feeling merely become a habit or was it a genuine premonition of more heartache to come?

I shivered and re-entered our apartment to finish packing. *Thank God, I'll be staying with our pastor and his wife until my tiny apartment is ready,* I thought gratefully. I was already lonely.

LOVE OFFERINGS

As I packed my clothes, I recalled how we had driven the short distance from Uncle John's to Turlock in search of a church. We believed the words written in the Bible: "And let us not neglect our meeting together, as some people do, but encourage one another..." (Hebrews 10:25). Shortly after joining that small church, we had moved into this tiny furnished two-bedroom apartment. Scraping up enough money for the usual moving-in costs, we'd had little left over. When the doorbell rang later the same day of our move, we were overwhelmed to see several friends from the church holding large boxes of food. Not only did they contain necessary staples, but also fresh and frozen cartons of meat. Our eyes widened as we took out packages of pork chops, ground beef, wieners, and even steaks—meats that we'd not had for a long time. Every now and then during the rest of our time there, different church members appeared with more edible love offerings—just at the moment when there was little in our refrigerator and pantry.

Ours was a little church in the midst of a small farming community, and none of its members were wealthy. But it was here that I learned how to give. Oh, I had given canned goods during food drives for the poor in our large church back in Texas. I had felt warm and fuzzy over donating the cans I had carefully selected from our pantry: cranberry sauce left over from the last holiday, beets, sauerkraut, all the off-brand items that I didn't really care about anyway. Stuff we wouldn't miss. But that wasn't giving.

As I finished packing after my mother drove away, I began to understand why God wanted us to become part of a local church family. We needed the love and nurture we received from it—in every way. Though our physical needs were important, our spiritual development needed to experience the laying aside of our fierce pride and accepting from others what they gave in love. As gratitude slowly replaced our pride, our feelings of shame lessened.

The church also needed us. It needed an outlet to experience the joy of giving as expressed by Jesus when He said, "When you did it to one of the least of these my brothers and sisters, you were doing it to me!" (Matthew 25:40). *Thank you, God, for leading us to this church and to Pastor Whitaker and his family. Without them, I would feel like an orphan right now. And thank you for their son, Don.*

~

Don and I had started dating shortly after we joined the church. He was tall and handsome, with dark wavy hair and clear blue eyes. I had assumed he was in college when he said that he was "in school." I felt uncomfortable when I later learned that he was only sixteen (I was nineteen), but because he was so mature, the age difference didn't prevent us from enjoying each other's company. We dated often, and he became like a member of our family. His sense of humor and unselfish willingness to always help brightened our days. He had his own car, which was a godsend for us when one day we found ourselves suddenly without transportation.

Shortly after I started working at the *Turlock Daily Journal* and Mom was working for the Collins family, we went out one morning to get into our car—but it wasn't where we had parked it. There was no garage or carport with our apartment, so we had to park it on the street. "Our car has been stolen!" Mom shouted into the phone minutes later to the police. I listened as she gave the necessary information. Suddenly she paled. "What do you mean it has been 'repossessed'? That car was paid for with cash. Not a penny was owed on it!"

But there was nothing we could do. The car was in Dad's name. We learned later that Dad had taken out a loan against it and deliberately missed the payments so it would be repossessed.

Mother had put $2,000 on that car. After a grocery-store worker had dropped a huge commercial-size can on her size four foot and she had undergone months of painful treatment, she was given $2,000 as a settlement. And I put $500 of my own money in on it since I knew I would be using it. I complained, "And we are letting him have the house and everything else. How could he do that?"

"We're not 'letting' him have anything, honey. The car is in his name, as is the house and everything back there. We have nothing," Mother said, in a matter-of-fact tone.

~

I slammed some books into a box, anger flaring again. *Lord, I still get mad when I think about that. There we were, barely surviving, and stranded. No money, no car, and no way to get to work. What a dirty trick! And yet, I thank You that You helped us find an old used car to get around in.*

I lugged the largest suitcase out to the street and opened the trunk of the car. *And thank You, Lord, that Don is so handy with cars and helped us keep this clunker running.*

I packed the last of my things into the car and was thankful again for the Whitaker family. Pastor Whitaker and his wife had invited me to stay with them for as long as I needed. It would be temporary, however, as the tiny apartment I had rented would be ready in two weeks. My plan was to continue working at the newspaper and save my money until fall, when I would enroll in college. I knew I'd have to work my way through school, but, with God's help, I was ready to do whatever was necessary.

The tantalizing aroma of pot roast welcomed me as I entered the parsonage carrying my meager belongings. "Ma" Whitaker opened her arms and hugged me as "Pa" grabbed my belongings and whisked them away to my room. I always felt relaxed in this godly home, where I was enveloped by an atmosphere of love so strong that it felt almost tangible. Despite my peaceful surroundings, however, I worried about Mom and the kids and didn't sleep well that first night.

I awoke early the next day, exhausted and weary, but managed to drag myself to work. Several days later, my mood matched the weather that dreary, foggy early January morning but I forced myself to concentrate on my job. I had recently been promoted and trained as one of three Linotype operators at the newspaper. One of the operators had injured her wrist over the weekend, so that left the typing of the entire daily newspaper to the other operator and me. It was a hectic day, leaving little time for me to dwell on the growing uneasiness in the pit of my stomach.

Shortly after dinner that evening, I excused myself and retired to my room. *I'm glad Don is spending the night with a buddy,* I thought gratefully. *I am so exhausted, I don't even have the energy to be sociable.* I dropped into my bed and quickly fell into a deep sleep.

A PREMONITION FULFILLED

In the early morning hours, the jangling of the pastor's phone in his study across the hall from my bedroom jarred the stillness. I forced myself to rise and open my bedroom door slightly. I heard the pastor's voice when he finally answered, but his words were inaudible. I froze with fear, for I knew it was bad news. Perched on the edge of my bed, I shivered and waited, like a tiny bird bracing itself for an approaching storm.

The pastor rapped softly on my now-open door. Placing his hand on my shoulder, he said gently, "It's your Aunt Eunice. She has some bad news." Eunice was my granny's sister, one of our closest relatives living across town from us. My throat suddenly closed. I was barely able to speak into the phone.

"Kitty," Aunt Eunice said gently, "your mom is in the hospital. Your dad tried to kill her and she is not expected to live."

"Oh, no!" I gasped. "Did he shoot her?"

My great-aunt hesitated, trying to arrange unarrangeable words. "No, honey," she said. "I'm so sorry to have to tell you this... ." Fighting for control, she finally sobbed out, "He beat her in the head with a claw hammer while the children were sleeping in the back of the house."

"A claw hammer!" Pain seared my mind as it focused on the mental images burning into it.

The children! "What about the—?"

"Chuck and Chris are safe here with us. We don't know where your dad is. There is an APB out on him, and the police in Turlock have been alerted—we're afraid he might come after you next. I'll call you tomorrow when we learn more."

After I stammered goodbye, my pastor and his wife led me back to my room, where I sobbed out the news. Their faces reflected the horror

I felt, but they remained silent until I finished. They gathered me gently into their arms. I felt one with them as their bodies shook with soundless sobs. We knelt and prayed for my mom and for the terrified children. They prayed that my father would be found before further harm was done. They prayed for me, that I would be granted peace, strength, and wisdom to endure this painful moment and the difficult times that lie ahead. I relaxed in the warmth of their love. It comforted me to know that they would continue praying for me through the night. I knew there would be no rest for any of us.

"Please, God, don't let Mom die!" I prayed as I curled into a tight ball in my bed.

The next day Aunt Eunice called with an update. "Your dad was arrested and is in the same hospital as your mom. He apparently took an overdose of something and was found semiconscious early this morning in his car parked near the entrance of the waterworks. He was found by an employee on his way to work."

How convenient! I thought. *He's always thinking. Let him die, Lord—he doesn't deserve to live.*

My aunt continued, "Your mother is awake and is calling for you."

Oh, thank You, God. She is still alive!

"The children are okay, but I think they've come down with the measles."

The measles! Lord, you let them come down with the measles?

"Oh, no. Poor things—as if they're not in enough misery already." I asked to speak to them but they had been quarantined to one room. My Aunt Eunice and Uncle Henry lived with their oldest daughter and her husband. "Tell Chuck and Chris that I love them and I miss them. I'll be there as soon as I can."

I collected my paycheck, tied up all the loose ends, said tearful good-byes to the Whitakers, and boarded a train to Los Angeles. During the trip, however, my train was detained for an hour due to the derailment of another train, caused by bad weather. As a result, I missed my connection with the new, streamlined Sunset Limited in Los Angeles. I had a three-hour wait in the large, cold Union Station.

It was already dark by the time I finally boarded what some of the passengers called "the milk train." The train was old, cold, and rickety. I soon discovered it would shuffle to a stop at every tiny town it happened upon. I found an empty row of seats and settled into one.

I slept fitfully during the night, until I was awakened in the early hours of the morning by cold drops of water falling on my head. It was raining and there was a leak above me, so I changed seats. The next morning, I stared gloomily out the window as the rain drenched the gray, barren thirsty desert. Trickles of water ran with force down the outside of the glass. As we passed a large desert bush, I noted a drenched cottontail hunching beneath it for shelter. *Lord, I feel as desolate as that little rabbit. Help us both. But most of all, help Mom. Please let her be alive when I get there.*

Aunt Eunice and my cousins met me at the train depot. "Is Mom..." My throat tightened. I couldn't finish the question.

"She's alive, and she's still asking for you." They whisked me quickly to the hospital.

When I entered Mom's room, I saw Granny sitting by Mom's bedside, where she had been day and night since her arrival. She arose quickly and hugged me hard.

"Thank You, God, for bringing Kitty here safely," she whispered. I clung to her and kissed her soft, wrinkled face, wet with tears of joy at my arrival.

Granny always did cry easily. We used to tease her about her free-flowing tears. Always when we arrived at our step-grandfather McAllister's farm, Granny would descend upon us, mouth quivering and tears flowing. "Why are you crying, Granny?" we'd say through the rolled-down windows. "Aren't you happy to see us?" we'd laughingly ask, knowing the answer.

"Yes, I'm happy to see you, but I don't want you to leave."

Tumbling out of the car we would hug her and say, "Granny, we're not leaving, we're arriving."

"I know," she'd respond sheepishly. "But you're going to be leaving in a week."

I turned toward Mom's bed. I don't know what I expected, but I wasn't prepared for what I saw. Swathed in bandages from the neck up, her head swollen to twice its normal size, Mom looked like a gigantic mummy from a horror movie. There were only slits for her eyes, nose, and mouth.

"Oh, Mom," I cried, rushing to her. Though it was difficult for her to speak, little by little she filled me in on what happened that fateful night.

After the children went to bed, Mom said she had developed a sudden, severe headache. Dad gave her a pill for her discomfort that we later learned was a "yellow jacket"—something to knock her out completely. He had wanted no interruptions while he carried out the diabolical plan he had formed before he went to California and brought her back. Once she was asleep, Dad took a claw hammer and methodically beat her in the head and temples until he thought she was dead. He then quietly left the house and drove away.

In the early morning hours, Mom regained consciousness. Her eyes were swollen shut and she couldn't see. She wondered why she felt wet and sticky over her entire body. She knew it wasn't sweat—it was too thick. Besides, it was winter.

Something is terribly wrong, she thought. She believed that whatever it was, my dad was the cause of it. The house was deathly quiet, but she wasn't sure he was gone. She slowly felt her way to the telephone and dialed the operator. Speaking distinctly and calmly, she said almost in a whisper, "Please send an ambulance—I think I am dying."

Worried about the children, she groped her way back to Chuck's room. Nudging him awake, she whispered in the darkness, "Go wake your sister. We've got to leave. And don't turn on the light."

"But what . . .?"

"Shhh. I don't know where your dad is, but something is wrong. Go to Chris's room and get her. We're going to the hospital."

"The hospital?"

"Just go get her, honey. Hurry!"

Chuck returned shortly with Chris stumbling behind in the dark. Mom grabbed their hands, and the three of them padded softly into the living room. When the harsh yellow of the outside streetlight fell across Mom through the window,

Chris started screaming. To her, Mom appeared as a crimson, slimy monster. Chuck, horrified by what he saw, froze into a speechless statue.

Mother was bloody from head to foot. Her blood-soaked gown clung to her thin body. Puffed eyelids protruded from her face, already swollen shut beyond recognition. Fearing for their lives, Mom again shushed them to be quiet. Minutes later the ambulance came and transported them to the hospital.

"You know the rest of the story, honey," Mom said weakly. I squeezed her hand and insisted she rest. I feared she had overdone it. *I shouldn't have let her talk so much,* I chided myself.

"We'll talk more tomorrow, but for now you need your rest, Mom. I love you so much. I don't know what I would do without you. You will come through this. God will help you and so will the rest of us."

Suddenly, I felt exhausted. I slid into an empty chair near Granny, close enough to Mom's bed to still hold her hand. Granny arose and tucked the covers in around Mom. We sat there in silence until we heard Mother's even breathing.

As Mom continued to hover between life and death, the doctors sadly explained to Granny and me that it was not likely she would survive. They were trying to prepare us for what they believed was the inevitable, but we both kept praying for a miracle.

(We learned later from the ambulance drivers who visited Mom at our home after her release from the hospital that the medical staff on duty in the ER the night they brought her in didn't give Mom a blood transfusion. They were short on blood and firmly believed it was impossible for her to survive.)

Thus it was that I again became a supporting member of my hurting family.

CHAPTER SIX

The Painful Path

I don't know why, but I kept thinking of Dad lying in his hospital bed on the floor just above us. Like the tongue is drawn irresistibly to the empty socket of a missing tooth, my mind returned to the idea of sneaking up and taking a peek into Dad's room. I didn't want to talk with him, nor did I want him to see me, but for some strange reason, I wanted to go to his room and observe him unnoticed. The idea wouldn't go away.

My second day there, I took the elevator up to Dad's floor and located his room. The chair next to the wall just outside his room was empty. *The guard must be taking a break*, I thought gratefully. I didn't want anyone to know I was there.

If Dad's awake, I decided, *I'll just step back and not enter. Lord, please let him be asleep.* I peeked through the partially open door. Dad's head rested on a pillow, his face turned slightly toward the opposite wall. Holding my breath,

I inched the door open a little wider. I was relieved when I saw his mouth open in deep sleep. He was unshaven, and his wavy brown hair, which he took such pride in, was tousled and looked dirty. Both wrists were chained to the metal frame of his bed.

He's chained there like a wild, helpless, dirty animal! I thought. Sudden pity flooded my heart. *How sad!*

But the feeling lasted only for a moment. My emotions then ran rampant.

Feelings of anger and hate wrestled with pity and disgust deep within me. Good memories and bad memories jostled in a mind that didn't know what to think. Past scenes of my childhood played across the screen of my mind—times when I crawled into Dad's lap, plying him with hugs and kisses, trying to draw from him something that would fill the emptiness of my childish heart for at least a moment. *I will be so good and loving that he will stop being bad and he will love me!* my childish mind had vowed. But my love wasn't strong enough to change him into a good father.

I recalled how, despite my fear and hate for him at times, as I grew older, my hungry heart pushed me to try and elicit affection from him verbally. "Do you love me, Daddy?"

Most often he responded irritably with, "What do you think? I go to work every day to provide you with food, clothing, and a place to live. Doesn't that show you that I love you?"

No, it didn't. That wasn't enough. As I grew older, I recalled thinking, *Would he stop working and doing all those things if he didn't love me? And what about the way he treats us? If he really loved us, why was he so mean?* Ultimately, I gave in to frustration and decided *I don't know why I even care!*

There had been happy times when Dad made us laugh, when he was demonstrative, but they were overshadowed by our fear. We could only enjoy those moments guardedly. We realized they would soon be buried beneath more layers of hurt, distrust, and fear, for we knew the good moments wouldn't last.

I don't know how long I stood there gazing at the man who was not only my father but also my enemy. *How can this be, Lord? I don't know what to feel. Do I hate him or do I pity him? My heart is numb. I feel like I should pray right now—but I don't know what to say. Please help me.*

I tiptoed to the door and peered out. The guard's chair was still empty.

Several days later Dad was discharged and taken to jail.

THE SCENE OF THE SHADOW OF DEATH

One of my most difficult duties was to return to our home. A friend drove me there and, at my insistence, continued on to do her grocery shopping. For some strange reason, I wanted to be alone. Was it because I was ashamed for anyone else to see evidence of that night's horror? Was this just another in succession of a lifelong line of duties that I alone felt responsible for carrying out?

Accompanied only by the tall, leafless oak trees, twisted, ugly, and grotesque in their nakedness as they loomed over me in the front yard, I stood on the front walk and waited.

For what?

Am I ready to face what I will see inside?

I shivered as I fumbled with the key in the lock, dreading the moment of entry.

The living room looked much the same, except for some clutter. Newspapers lay scattered on the coffee table and floor. But it was eerie as I entered the dining room. A huge pot of Mother's delicious homemade stew, now caked and hard, sat in the middle of the table. Dishes with crusty, partially eaten food were still in their places. Dirty glasses, some with curdled, dry milk, stood by their plates. It was as though everyone were suddenly whisked away.

The rest of the rooms were chaotic, with drawers open, some partially empty on the floor, and their contents strewn about. Disarray was everywhere—exactly as the investigative officers had left things in their search for clues behind this horrendous crime. Clues had been found in letters that Dad had written to someone, we never learned who, which described his plan to murder Mom. This evidence led to his charge of premeditated attempted murder.

The last room—and the hardest for me to enter—was the scene of the crime, my mom and dad's bedroom. I stood before the closed door, trembling, suddenly afraid to touch the knob. Was I really prepared for what was on the other side? Could I handle it even with God's help? I wasn't sure. I took a deep breath, slowly turned the knob, and gently pushed open the door.

The bed and all its gore loomed in full view. The rumpled sheets and pillows were a tangled mass of stiff, bloodied fabric. The sheer white curtain panels on the window near the bed, mute witnesses to the room's horror, bore a macabre pattern of random dark blotches running from their top ruffle down to the floor. Magenta marks tracked back and forth across the floral patterned carpet. Crimson stains, stark against the pale white embossed wallpaper, streaked upward onto the ceiling. With wide, unblinking eyes, I followed the path of the stain's ultimate destination onto the vaulted ceiling. I caught my breath as the viciousness of the attack penetrated my dumfounded mind. *These walls are ten feet high!*

The bedspread, blankets, and quilts were folded back at the end of the bed and showed only minimal evidence of what took place. It struck me as strange that such care would be taken to spare bedclothes the same carnage that was planned for the bed's inhabitant. My mom. I fell against the wall, sobbing.

Lord, I don't know if I can do this. Please give me strength to clean all of this up, I prayed. I knew Chuck would have helped me, but though he was a teenager, I still thought of him and protected him as a child—my child.

No, I decided, *I will do this alone. The children would be horrified by this scene. They have been through enough. But as I clean everything up, Lord, please don't let me be consumed with hate for my father.*

It took several trips to do what must be done and put everything back into place. Each trip was an exercise in faith, determination, and prayer. Finally, with a power that came only from God, everything was ready for our return.

Our first night home was difficult. I asked Chris to sleep with me until she felt secure enough to sleep alone. I feared that her recurring nightmares of that terrible night and her ride in the ambulance might worsen.

For some strange reason, the ambulance drivers had placed Chuck in the front with them, and left Chris, the youngest, to ride alone in the back of the ambulance where Mom was securely strapped to the gurney. Chris had been terrified. When Mom suddenly became motionless and didn't respond, little Chris thought her mother had died.

She watched in silent terror as her mother's still form swayed eerily with every motion of the ambulance. With each turn, the gurney swayed into Chris and jostled her. Her mother's blood dripped onto Chris's nightclothes, frightening her even more.

Chris will need to sleep with me a long time, I decided.

And maybe, deep inside, I needed her company.

~

I prayed for continued strength and wisdom as I dealt with our everyday problems. Besides spending most of each day with Mom at the hospital, I filled out medical insurance forms and dealt with living expenses. Our house was paid for, but we had no income. The savings account had been cleaned out and there was no checking account. All we had to live on was the money I had brought with me and a little Granny had forced me to take. She and Grandpa McAllister had very little, and they struggled to survive on their rocky-soiled farm. Fortunately, the owner of the newspaper in Turlock had given me some extra money out of his pocket when I left, as had the Whitakers. *I have to find a job soon,* I worried, *but that's not going to be easy.* The family car had been impounded for evidence when Dad was arrested, and I had no transportation. With the kind help of many wonderful friends, neighbors, and a good bus system, I was able to get around. Soon I found work and brought in enough money for us to survive.

One morning, as I stood at the bus stop in freezing rain, I saw our family car go by with someone whom I didn't recognize at the wheel. After arriving at work, I called the sheriff's department and was told it was still impounded. When I explained that I had just seen it, they said I was mistaken. We later learned that it had been sold—to someone in the sheriff's department. I had forgotten that the car was still in my father's name. Dad had used the money from its sale to hire a private attorney. He didn't want to use the one appointed by the court. (Following the trial, Dad's attorney forced us to pay $300 for the deed to our house, which Dad had given him, even though the court had awarded the house to us.)

~

After twenty-six long, painful days, Mom was discharged from the hospital. One of the doctors admitted, "We had little to do with her survival—it was obviously the work of God." We rejoiced upon her discharge, but shortly after arriving home she developed lockjaw. For weeks, the only nutrition she received was through a straw. She ultimately overcame that discomfort, but her private pain—physical and mental—would continue for a lifetime.

Dad's stay in the hospital had been very brief. We were convinced that his "overdose" had been merely a sympathy-getting ploy to lay groundwork for his temporary insanity plea, which we were certain he would use. Shortly after he was transported to jail, he was released on bail with instructions not to leave the state. His freedom, however, made us again his prisoners.

We nailed our windows shut and put deadbolts on our doors. Despite these precautions, we were still afraid to go to sleep at night. With no air conditioning and only small fans to rearrange the hot air, the humid Texas nights were almost unbearable.

I found a better-paying job as a night proofreader for our city's local *Gazette* and began dating Floyd Moore, a co-worker who had graduated from my high school the same year as I. Floyd was one of the most thoughtful and considerate young men I had ever known. He provided me with transportation, not only to and from work, but to countless other places necessitated by daily living. He also had friends on the police force who were kind and concerned enough to patrol the front and back of our house day and night, on and off duty.

I enjoyed Floyd's company and admired his integrity. I knew he cared for me deeply, and the fact that I didn't feel the same way toward him added guilt to my burdens. *I wish I could fall in love with Floyd. He has all of the attributes I admire in a man. He would make a wonderful husband,* I often thought. *Maybe in time, I will,* I hoped. Floyd was a blessing from God during that difficult time of my life. Though he would always have a special place in my heart, he was not the man I was to marry.

~

Each time we made the trip to the courthouse, emotionally prepared for the ordeal of Dad's trial, we left disappointed and angry. Dad's attorney always appeared without our father, stating that Dad was "sick." It seemed this frustrating chapter in our lives would never end.

In reality, Dad was never sick. He was out of state. We children began receiving letters from him postmarked in California. Though he never wrote Mother, we knew these letters were written for her benefit. They were sickeningly sweet, telling us how much he loved and missed us. One letter included photos of him at the beach with three scantily clad attractive young women clinging to him.

"Aren't my girlfriends cute?" his handwriting taunted from the back of one photo. One letter addressed to me contained three ten-dollar bills—the only money we ever received from him. He said it was for us children to spend on something "fun" for ourselves. When I showed Mom the letter, she crumpled the bills, threw them on the floor, and stomped on them. She then calmly picked them up, smoothed them out, and we used them for groceries.

Several weeks later, we learned that Dad had returned from California. There were rumors that he was going out of his way to be friendly, looking up old family friends, shaking hands with everyone he had known, seen, or met, as though he were on a political campaign trail. He encountered Granny one day at the bus station, just as she arrived in town, where he loudly begged her forgiveness for his "one mistake" to her daughter. When he extended his hand, Granny snarled, "Do you really think I would shake your hand! Get away from me."

Finally, five months following Mom's discharge from the hospital, Dad appeared in court for his trial. We weren't surprised at Dad's temporary insanity plea, but we were surprised by the method he used to substantiate it. And we weren't prepared for the humiliation it would bring.

The defense stated that my mother and I were prostitutes in our home. Dad was depicted as a devoted family man who came home early one night and caught his wife in bed with another man. That was shocking enough, they said, but when he learned that his beautiful daughter was also a prostitute, he was devastated and blamed his wife for her bad example. (Strangely, that was the first time I ever heard my father describe me as beautiful. I grew up hearing him call me ugly and stupid.) The defense explained that when the defendant stumbled upon the dirty truth he simply couldn't handle it. He became so distraught that he committed this crime—for which he was now "deeply sorry."

After the defense set the perfect stage for his entrance, Dad gave a flawless performance on the stand—even to the point where he broke into sobs after uttering the sad words, "And that's how I found out about the immoral activities of my sweet wife and precious daughter."

We were torn by the injustice of the situation. It seemed that we, the victims, were now on trial as everyone in the packed courtroom turned and glared at us. A parade of character witnesses for my dad flocked to the stand and declared his goodness under oath, stating that he was "incapable of hurting a fly."

These were sincere people who really believed what they were saying. Many of them had known or worked closely with my father for ten years. But they had no way of knowing what he was really like. They saw only what my father wanted them to see. Besides, who wouldn't believe such a kind-appearing man, head in hands, sobbing, obviously heartbroken over the tragic turn of events in his life?

When the reality of the defense's statement penetrated my mind, a feeling of hot shame suddenly poured over me. As a young woman who had never "known a man" in the biblical sense, such an accusation was unbearable. And how my heart ached for my mother. *Poor little Mom! This is adding insult to injury! How can they lie like this in court and get away with it?*

Everything that followed appeared in silent slow motion. I saw my tiny granny rise to her feet and cry out, "That is a filthy lie!" but my numb mind heard nothing. I saw the judge pound his gavel and call out "order in the court," but I heard no sound. I watched my granny's lips move again and the judge threaten to have her removed from the courtroom if there were further outbursts. I was suspended, frozen within a sphere of soundless, silent pain, one that would haunt me for years.

The people subpoenaed in our behalf, friends who were to declare to the world our good character, never appeared. The pastor of our church, who had given Mom a bad reference while we were in Turlock, had left the area before our return, so I again attended the same church, where I was loved and supported by some of my close friends there. But it hurt that not one of them or any of our other friends appeared in court to support us. We learned later that they didn't want to "be involved."

Even more painful were the remarks later made by an acquaintance, who said, "Well, where there's smoke there's bound to be fire. Why would your own father lie about something like that?" Someone else commented, "Well, your mom must have enjoyed being knocked around, otherwise she wouldn't have stayed with him all those years."

Though I was deeply hurt, I understood. How could I expect outsiders to look beyond the persuasive powers of my charismatic father? And how could I expect ignorant people, who knew nothing about the helpless feelings of battered women, to understand?

After five hours of deliberation, the jury finally convicted my father of premeditated attempted murder and sentenced him to three-and-a-half years in prison.

Since the maximum sentence for premeditated attempted murder at that time in Texas was fifteen years, we felt humiliation rather than vindication. It was apparent that the jury believed Dad was guilty—there was too much evidence substantiating his crime—but some of them obviously also believed what was said about Mom and me. Out of sympathy for the defendant, they had given him the minimum sentence.

Though we stung from that light sentence, we were thankful that Dad had been convicted, even for a short time. At last we were free.

Chapter Seven

Don't Ask Me to Forgive!

Following Dad's trial, he threatened to "get us" upon his release. He blamed us for his conviction and vowed to make us pay someday. But we were free now—at least for three-and-a-half years. Maybe less, depending upon the parole board. We would later learn that he was released six months early due to good behavior. Would he find us after his release? Would we have to keep running?

We pushed his threats to the back of our mind as we put our house up for sale and made our plans to move to California. Mom and I excitedly looked up information about the Golden State. We didn't want to move too close to relatives because we didn't want to be a burden, yet we wanted to live close enough to visit them from time to time. We loved the ocean, but we also loved the mountains. We wanted to live in a city that wasn't too large, yet was big enough to provide employment opportunities. Where could we find such a perfect place?

Despite our newfound freedom from fear, I wasn't happy. Fear had disappeared, but anger spread quickly to fill its place. I was growing angrier each day.

One morning, as I was sorting through the things I would either take or get rid of, I recalled the first time we had fled to California and how frustrated I was at having to decide what to take or leave behind. I recalled how I, as the oldest child, had assumed an unrealistic responsibility for my siblings and mother when I was very young—a burden far too heavy for the small shoulders of a child. *And it still seems too heavy,* I thought, my anger flaring.

Dad has caused me a lot of pain! I thought, tossing some items into the "for rummage" box. *Not only did he force adult burdens on me, he robbed me of the love and security every child should experience. Instead, I lived in constant fear—fear that he would find us, and fear of what would happen when he did find us. Will I always have to live in fear?* Not even the loving arms of the man I married two years later could protect me from recurring nightmares of Dad chasing me with a gun.

I was also angry because of the shame I felt that day in the courtroom when Mom and I had been called prostitutes in front of strangers. It would be years before I could watch a trial scene on television or in a movie without leaving the room in tears.

Though I loved the Lord and had continued to worship Him at the church where we were all baptized, bitter weeds of resentment sprang up rapidly in the fertile soil of my anger. *My father has caused every pain in my life, and he is still causing me problems. It's not fair,* I decided, kicking an empty box into the corner.

I didn't realize it then, but the anger I harbored was destructive. If I continued this line of thinking, my thoughts would develop patterns that would spread tenacious roots into every nook and cranny of my mind. If left unchecked and allowed to grow, they would produce fruit of their own kind, tempting fruit that, once tasted, could lure me into a vicious mental cycle. For, oh, how sweet are those first few bites of the victim mentality.

With the mind-set of a victim, even if I never saw my father again, I could blame him for all of life's difficulties. I could develop the habit of blaming others for all of life's problems and thus avoid responsibility for my own actions. I could eventually even blame God for dealing me such a bad hand. After all, why should I be held accountable for anything in life? I was born a victim and I would always be a victim.

But God had different plans. Once again, He sent someone to help me.

Not long after Dad was sent to prison, an older woman at church asked me, "Have you forgiven your father?"

I was shocked. *Forgive my father! My emotional wounds are still raw and bleeding; how dare you speak to me about forgiveness!*

"My father will never ask me to forgive him for anything—so I don't think I'll have to worry about that," I said crisply.

Her eyes were gentle and her voice soft as she said, "You may be right—but you still need to forgive him."

"Why should I do that?" I snapped. "He doesn't deserve forgiveness."

"Again, you are right, but you still need to forgive him."

"I'd like to know just who, in his right mind (*since I'm sure you aren't in yours*) would expect me to forgive my father after all he has done to us!"

She was quiet for a long moment. Finally she answered, "God."

I said nothing more, but inwardly I seethed. *Had she gone through what my family had, she wouldn't be standing there in her unscarred composure blithely advising me to forgive!* The scars on my mother's temples were still swollen, red, and angry—just like the anger swelling within me. *And I was supposed to think about forgiveness?*

I was irritated, but I wasn't going to let her unrealistic statements about forgiveness dampen my enthusiasm for our upcoming family move.

We were excited! Our spunky mother obtained her driver's license, and after the sale of our house we bought an inexpensive new car and a used trailer to haul what household items we would take with us. Soon we would be heading west to the beautiful state of California, which had everything: mild climate, azure blue ocean, warm sand, green valleys, the beautiful Sierra mountains, crystal clear streams, lots of job opportunities, and a new beginning. Not to mention Disneyland and Fisherman's Wharf.

But the woman's comments about forgiveness sharpened the teeth of conviction that continued to nip at me. I knew I needed to forgive Dad, but I wasn't ready to let go of my resentment. Not yet. *Soon we'll be gone and I won't be reminded of her comments because I'll never see her again,* I consoled myself. So I pushed it to the back of my mind.

Despite my resolve to not think about the forgiveness issue, from time to time it popped into my mind. And I argued, *My father doesn't deserve my forgiveness. What he really deserves is something worse than what he got! Only three-and-a-half years for premeditated attempted mur-*

der! If anyone has a right to hate and resent, it's my family and me.

GOD NEVER GIVES UP

But I had a problem. I knew that the Bible had much to say about forgiveness. Though I read my Bible diligently, I picked and chose the truths I wanted to relate to and ignored the ones I didn't want to deal with. I loved reading about the "goodies" in the Bible—how much God loves me, how He would never leave me nor forsake me, and how nothing on earth could separate me from His love. Those were great verses!

I rejoiced over the verses that talked about how all the "bad" guys were going to "get it," how they would one day stand before God and then finally pay for their wrongdoings. The only problem with those verses was that I didn't want to wait until some future day of judgment. I wanted to see them get what was due them *now*. Besides, why should I concern myself about forgiving someone who had not yet even begun to pay for his wrongs?

I knew, however, that this special relationship between my heavenly Father and me was never meant to be one-sided. The Bible made it clear that Christ was not only my Savior and friend, He was also my Lord. As my friend, I knew He would encourage and comfort me through all the rough spots in life. I also knew a real friend would never lie to me. Christ would always guide me toward honesty and truth, even when I tried to hide behind a wall of denial.

I didn't need great spiritual wisdom to understand that God is not someone to call just to help me out of jams. God was not created for me; I was created for Him. And once I accepted Him as Lord of my life, He expected me to trust His wisdom and obey Him in every area of life, even when I didn't understand. This included forgiving others. Specifically, my father.

Deep in my heart, I wanted to live up to God's expectations of me by doing my part. The problem was, I wanted to choose which parts. The easy parts. So, I focused mostly on the "thou shalt nots." Not bow down to any false gods? Why would I do that? I had a relationship with the living God!

Not take God's name in vain? Remember the Sabbath, and honor my father and mother? No problem there. I'd never developed the habit of swearing, I enjoyed going to church, and I loved and respected my mother. I didn't respect my father, of course, but with God's help I had treated him with respect.

Not kill anyone? Well...when I accepted Christ into my life that desire went away. After all, I had never really *wanted* to kill my father, I just wanted him to stop hurting us.

Not commit fornication or adultery? Of course, I had been tempted in that area, but my mind was made up. I definitely was going to remain sexually chaste until my wedding day. After all, it was my choice.

Not steal from my neighbor? Piece of cake. I didn't have a problem in that area even before I was a Christian (not unless you count stealing flowers from the neighbor's yard).

Not covet what my neighbors had? No problem there. I may have wanted some things just like what they had but I never wanted *theirs*.

Yes, my score seemed pretty good in the Old Testament "thou shalt not" category!

But what about the New Testament commandment summarization by Jesus when He said, "You must love the Lord your God with all your heart, all your soul, and all your mind" and "Love your neighbor as yourself" (Matthew 22:37,39). It was a lot easier to not do the things I wasn't supposed to do than to do the things I was *supposed* to do.

God had a way of nudging my thoughts to the "thou shalt" Scriptures—the verses that tell us to forgive those who wrong us, to love our enemies and pray for them, to bless those who persecute us, and to be accountable for our own actions, which included even our thoughts. Those were the tough ones!

The closest I ever wanted to get to praying for those who wronged me was similar to that of an old Yiddish prayer I once heard. In this prayer a man prayed, "God, bless the man I hate with a million dollars—and may he give it all to the doctors."

Choosing my thoughts, much less controlling them, seemed impossible. I equated thoughts with feelings, which somehow just happened and you couldn't help them. As my thoughts continued to wrestle with the subject of forgiveness, however, I realized I again had to make a choice.

Two paths stretched before me. I could choose the path of resentment and remain an embittered prisoner, or I could choose the path of forgiveness and be set free. But how could I find the strength to forgive my father when all that was within me screamed for vengeance?

Following my spiritual commitment six years earlier, I had formed the habit of consistently searching the Scriptures for anything that could help me survive my circumstances. Though I hadn't always understood their wisdom, nor always lived up to them, I had often proved their power as I applied their principles. Recalling the many times I had been able to do what the Scriptures encouraged me to do gave me hope that maybe I could also someday forgive my father.

Would God be a just God, I thought, *if He commanded me to do something that He knew was impossible for me to do—and then hold me accountable for not doing it? Surely not.* As I struggled with these thoughts one day, I recalled a remarkable event from my past. Something short of a miracle.

When I think of it, from a human standpoint, it seems impossible that a person could face death at gunpoint and not be overcome by fear. And yet, hadn't I been able to do that very thing the night Dad held his gun to my head and threatened to pull the trigger? God had given me faith that prevented fear at one of the most dramatic moments of my life. Could He not also give me the power to forgive? The answer had to be an unequivocal "yes!"

Well, then why hadn't He?

I didn't realize it then, but I was waiting for God to do something that He wasn't going to do. And God was waiting for me to do what only I could do. So we were at a stalemate. But God is patient. He has plenty of time.

CALIFORNIA OR BUST

Our spirits were high as we arrived at our California destination—Santa Barbara—a haven nestled between the rugged coastal mountains and the sparkling sea. As we drove down Highway 101, the early morning sun danced across the blue Pacific Ocean and highlighted the beach that beckoned to us with all its beauty.

Mom and I found work immediately—Mom as a nurse's aide at Cottage Hospital and I as a proofreader for the Santa Barbara *News Press.* Chuck and Chris were enrolled in school and we began our new life. For the first six months we lived in Bam's Auto Court. It was cramped for the seven of us—Mom, me, Chuck, Chris, Fluffy our white cat, and two canaries—but we were happy.

Our first week there, I located a church and became involved, but Mom refused to go. She had been so hurt by our Texas pastor's betrayal that she couldn't trust Christians. And I couldn't blame her. Though I attended church, I had my own problems. I didn't trust Christians either.

The rip that had started in the lining of my heart with our Texas pastor's betrayal widened when none of our Christian friends appeared in court to support us at the trial. The tear extended so deep and hurt so bad that I had made a vow: *I will go to church and serve the Lord because I love Him, but I will never let anyone get close to me again.*

I didn't blame God because of man's failures. Just as Dad's bad choices were not my fault, neither was it God's fault when His family members made wrong choices. I let a scab form over my heart—a scab of protection—as I again became involved in the church.

So I understood when Mother lashed out at me angrily as I wrote out my small tithe check each payday. "You're taking food right out of our mouths when you give money to those people down at that church! How can you be so callous?"

I knew she didn't understand, that I wasn't giving money to "people" or "that church"—I was only giving back to God what was due Him. But it still hurt, for I loved my mother dearly. Though our financial circumstances were difficult, I never missed paying my tithe. And we never went hungry.

For the most part, I was in good spirits because we were free. Yet my burden of resentment grew heavier. I continued to resist God's nudgings toward forgiveness. The more He nudged, the more I dug in my heels emotionally. And my anger grew.

Why is forgiveness such a big deal, Lord? I serve You faithfully. I am at church every time the door opens. Doesn't that count for anything? Can't You give me a little slack? We're not talking about some spur-of-the-moment solitary act of violence committed by someone who was drunk or high on drugs. My dad was cold sober all of those years. He knew exactly what he was doing! It's hard to forgive someone who is that mean. In fact, for me, it's impossible.

And I was right. As long as I chose not to forgive, forgiveness was impossible.

HALF THE BATTLE

One day, I recalled conversations with my mom that had occurred frequently throughout my childhood. After asking me to do something, I had often whined, "But I can't."

Mother, who despite all of her disadvantages had never let the word "can't" stop her from attempting anything worthwhile, asked, "Why can't you?"

"I don't know how. And besides, I don't want to—it's too hard."

Her response was always the same. "Honey, wanting to is half the battle."

I pondered the wisdom of her words. Could it be that the heavy burden of unforgiveness weighing upon me was not because of my inability to forgive, nor God's unwillingness to help me forgive, but because of my refusal to forgive? But why can't I want to forgive Dad?

Struggling with this issue, I realized I had misconceptions about forgiveness. I believed that forgiveness meant that the wrongs my dad had done would suddenly be okay, and that he should not be fully punished according to the law. I also feared that as forgiving Christians, we would have to allow Dad access to us after his release, despite our fears and a lifetime injunction legally forbidding him from coming near us. After all, if you forgive someone, I reasoned, doesn't that mean you must not withhold your presence from that person even if you knew he would kill you?

I also felt that my refusal to forgive Dad was part of his punishment. I would get even with him by not forgiving him—which was about as logical as taking rat poison and then waiting for the rat to die. I thought my Dad would suffer if I didn't forgive him. I was wrong—I was the one who suffered. I'm sure he never lost one night's sleep because of my resentment. But I had. I had tossed and turned many sleepless, miserable nights because the poison of hate was working to destroy me.

But why hadn't God helped me?

As I processed all of this, I realized that I had expected God to do something He will never do—wrestle me into forgiving against my will. I thought of forgiving merely because it was the "Christian thing to do," not because I wanted to forgive Dad.

Early one morning, before rushing off to work, I read with awe in the Bible the words spoken by Jesus from the bleakness of the cross:

"Father, forgive them." As I pondered the words, I glanced out my window. The sun, shining through the treetops, slowly turned the dew-drops on each blade of overgrown grass into tiny diamonds. They danced in brilliant colors as a gentle wind blew lightly across the yard. Just as the sun turned those dewdrops into something lovely, God's truth began to illuminate the dark areas of my heart with new understanding.

As painful and as humiliating as death on the cross was for Jesus, I concluded, He experienced it because He chose to—not because He had to. He chose to because He knew what the benefits of His painful obedience would be for all mankind. It was love for the Father and each of us that had kept Him there. Jesus was not a victim—it was His choice to be a sacrifice for us—and it was His choice to forgive. He wanted God's will more than His own.

My mind warmed as truth embraced it. God will always give us the power to do what will honor Him, but He will never force anyone to do anything. Just as He hadn't forced Jesus to the cross, He would never force me to forgive. I must sincerely want to. But how?

FATHER, MAY I?

For me it was a giant step that morning when I decided to want to forgive Dad. I prayed, *Lord, please help me to change my want to's. I'm being as honest as I know how right now. Due to the resentful feelings I've held for so long in my heart, I don't want to forgive my father and I know You won't force me. Yet my love for You and my desire to please You is stronger than my heart's desire to hold on to my bitterness. You have said that You would help us do anything that will make us a better person—if we ask for Your help. So I'm asking. Please help me to want to forgive my father.* This became my daily prayer.

I don't remember when it happened—weeks, maybe months later—but I will always remember how it happened. One day, like a gentle breeze blowing the sweet fragrance of honeysuckle blossoms through the still air of a moonlit night, a sudden desire to forgive my father enveloped me. The bitterness of my heart melted as I whispered, "I forgive you, Dad—for everything!" The cleansing tears of relief that followed washed away all of the rancid remnants of resentment.

Shortly afterwards, I also forgave those Christians in my Texas hometown whom I felt had let me down. Jesus healed the hole in my heart and peeled away the scab so I could again begin to trust. My painful experiences of betrayal evolved into a blessing, for I learned at an early age that there is a difference between trusting people and leaning our total emotional weight upon them. God is the only one we are to love and trust with all our heart, soul, body, mind, and strength 100 percent of the time, because He is the only one who will never let us down. If we lean too hard on others, we will likely fall down when they move, when they abandon or disappoint us. In our disillusionment, we will become bitter and distrusting. Let's face it, we are human. Each of us will disappoint someone at some time. We need to understand this and not be shocked when it happens. God understands this frailty of human nature, and so should we.

"Yet he was merciful and forgave their sins... Many a time he held back his anger and did not unleash his fury! For he remembered that they were merely mortal..." (Psalm 78:38-39). We will never fall if we remember that our anchor is not secured by flesh. It holds solid and secure only in the spiritual—in Christ.

"This confidence is like a strong and trustworthy anchor for our souls. It leads us through the curtain of heaven into God's inner sanctuary" (Hebrews 6:19). I didn't know then that when I forgave my father, it would open my heart to an ongoing power—a power that would enable me to forgive him one final time, at another tragic time and place.

Chapter Eight

Love's Bumpy Road

Mrs. Chappell beamed as she hurried toward me following the church service. "I want you to meet my son, Jerry," she called out.

She had spoken of her son for months, but he had never attended any of our services. I was choir director at our small church, and quite a few mothers dragged their sons to church to meet me. I suspected they were dangling me as an incentive to get their sons to take a more serious look at their spiritual needs. Mrs. Chappell was no exception.

I rarely dated anyone who was not a Christian. I firmly believed God's admonition: "Don't team up with those who are unbelievers...How can light live with darkness?" (2 Corinthians 6:14).

I knew that even the best marriages had their difficult moments, times when prayer and obedience to God were imperative to avoid the divorce court. My future husband and I must serve the same God, for how could I ask God to whisper His truths into my husband's heart if my husband's heart didn't belong to Him? To marry a nonbeliever would be like trying to mix oil and water.

This morning, however, Jerry stood beside her, blue eyes sparkling, his wavy auburn hair slicked back. We shook hands, but no sparks flew. I told him I hoped he would visit the church again, and he did. He asked me out for a Coke following an evening service, and we began dating. He was kind and gentle and fun to be with.

Several weeks later, while playing miniature golf, we drifted onto the subject of our plans for the future. "Once my family can make it without me," I said, lining my putter up behind the ball for a short putt, "I'd like to attend a Christian college in Riverside, major in music, and become a music director. Oh, rats!" I lamented, missing the hole. While Jerry made his putt, I continued. "That would be a disappointment to all of my aunts in the South, though—they're praying for me to find the 'right man' and get married. They say I'm an 'old maid.' "

"At twenty-two?" Jerry quipped, brows raised.

"Most of my high school friends married right after graduation," I explained.

Jerry laughed and said, "Well, you don't look like an old maid to me."

"I don't know what an old maid is supposed to look like, but I'll probably look even more like one by the time I do get married—which is a long way off. And my future husband must be a Christian." The last statement wasn't directed at Jerry, it was a matter-of-fact comment made to a good friend. I added Scripture to explain my position.

"I know what you mean," Jerry said. "Marriage isn't in my plans for a long time, either. I'm only an apprentice now, but soon I'm going to be a sheet metal journeyman and I'll make more money. I want to save up and one day start a business of my own."

He ignored my comments about my future husband's spiritual qualifications. There was no point since there was no romantic interest in our dating. We both relaxed and enjoyed our platonic friendship, secure in the belief that it would never lead to anything romantic.

During the following months, Jerry attended church regularly. One night God whispered to his heart, and he responded by inviting Christ into his life. The stage was now set for Cupid, whose aim was perfect. Jerry and I fell in love, but there was a problem. Jerry gave in to Cupid, but I resisted.

I wasn't consciously aware of my deep distrust of men. It was hidden deep in my soul, tucked away in a pocket of fear and incorrect assumptions. I should have noted the symptoms, but I didn't. Because of my background, I felt that God had somehow made a mistake when he created Adam. Oh, I believed that when Adam and Eve sinned, the rest of us inherited their disease, but I felt that the male gender inherited a greater dose. I suspected a serious flaw, a stronger genetic propensity for violence that was passed from Adam to all men—not women, just to men. I often asked myself, *Who starts wars, who rapes, pillages, and brutalizes people? It's men! Rarely does a woman do anything so terrible.* Though my ideas felt valid, the root of my problem was fear. But I didn't know it.

THE HARD-TO-SAY WORDS MYSTERY

Jerry and I enjoyed each other's company, and we laughed a lot. As our deep friendship grew, I relaxed, and the love began to grow in my heart. Jerry's love for me grew stronger, and when he asked me to marry him, I accepted. Strangely, when he told me he loved me, I could not respond wholeheartedly. I was barely able to stiffly say the words "Me too."

Why is it so hard for me to say those beautiful and romantic words? I wondered. *What's wrong with me?* It didn't make sense, for I knew I wanted to be with him. *Maybe I don't really love him,* I wondered. *If I don't, then why am I so miserable when I'm not with him?* I couldn't sort it all out at the time, but one thing I knew, I couldn't imagine life without Jerry.

I was excited the following Saturday afternoon when we drove to a wholesale jeweler in Oxnard and picked out a beautiful wedding ring set. During our celebration dinner, Jerry placed the engagement ring on my finger and again told me how much he loved me. I responded only with a kiss. I extended my hand so we could both admire the ring. The diamonds sparkled in the soft restaurant light.

As we both admired the ring encircling my finger, I stiffened with realization. A sharp feeling of bondage, braided into a steel-like band, looped itself around my heart and squeezed tightly. The suffocating depression I felt almost took my breath away.

Why am I depressed? I'm supposed to be happy, I wondered, shocked at the intensity of my feelings. I tried to shake them by discussing our upcoming wedding plans, but by the time we were in the car and driving home, I could barely breathe. I became quiet—very unusual for me. I lay down in the front seat and rested my head in Jerry's lap, so dejected I couldn't speak.

What have I done? I asked myself in shock.

I rubbed the ring, suddenly heavy on my finger, its significance now strangely unsettling. *This ring symbolizes a lifetime commitment. The same commitment that saying "I love you" brings,* I reminded myself. *You don't accept a ring and you don't say "I love you" unless you intend to give yourself, your heart, your body, your entire life to a man—forever!*

I lay there, rigid with fright, as my apprehensive thoughts escalated.

How do I know he won't become like my father once we are married? Sure, he says he has turned his life over to God, but my dad made the same claims. Jerry is all sweetness and love now—he wants me to marry him—but what about later, in the privacy of our marriage, when there's nobody but him and me? And I wouldn't count! I closed my eyes, but I couldn't shut out my fears.

I dozed from exhaustion and had flashbacks to when I was eleven years old.

After hearing Mom's screams early one evening, I ran through the open door into their bedroom. Mom was on her knees looking up at Dad, tears pouring down her face. Her raven hair was in disarray, most of it still in curlers. Dad stood above her, one large hair-covered curler still in his hand, roots and all. Mom's left hand covered the bleeding spot on her head, and through sobs she said, "One day I am going to hate you with the same fervor that I now love you."

Those words bore into my young psyche and branded my mind, never to be forgotten. At that moment I decided, *I don't ever want to love anyone that much! In fact, I don't ever want to love anyone, period!*

I was jerked back into the present when Jerry braced me with his hand as he braked the car, narrowly missing a truck that had changed lanes abruptly. Instinctively, I cringed at his touch.

What's wrong with me? I wondered again. As I lay there, hollow in heart, I didn't connect the dots. It wasn't until years later that I understood. All I knew at that moment was that I was suffocating with a feeling of oppression.

Jerry sensed my distress. He stroked my face with his right hand, his left still on the wheel, and asked, "What's wrong, honey? You seem unhappy."

"I am," I mumbled.

After a long pause, he asked, "Are you sorry that we are engaged?"

I started crying. "I don't know why, but, yes, I am."

How those words must have slashed his heart! But he answered gently, "Then you can give the ring back to me. We won't make this commitment just yet."

When we reached Santa Barbara, I took the ring off my finger and handed it to him. We hugged, he kissed me on the cheek, and left.

Entering the house, I felt free again. Like a butterfly that had just escaped its captor's net. My heart soared in freedom.

The following Saturday, Jerry made the long drive back to Oxnard by himself and returned the ring. The salesman said, "I've been in this business a long time, and I'm a good judge of people. I'm going to put this set aside because I know you two will be back."

THE ULTIMATUM

Jerry and I continued dating. I returned to my previously happy self, but Jerry appeared gaunt, sometimes withdrawn.

He laughed less, and the sparkle in his blue eyes was gone. One night, after returning from a date, Jerry and I sat on the couch talking. Mom, Chuck, and Chris were still out, involved in their own lives, and the house was quiet. Jerry took my hands, looked me in the eyes, and announced, "If you don't marry me, I am moving to a suburb near San Francisco. Remember my friend Dave who lives in Daley City? He's invited me to stay with him until I find a job."

My heart sank into a pit of shock and fear. *How can he just leave? I thought he loved me.* But I kept silent.

"When I walk out that door," he continued,

"I will walk out of your life forever. I love you very much, but I can't go on this way." He stood and walked slowly toward the door without looking back.

I sat there, disturbed by this new development. Once again, I had a life-changing choice to make. Would I let the man of my dreams walk out of my life forever because of some unexplained fear of commitment, or would I go after him?

Like a mute but seeing statue, I watched Jerry open the door, step outside, and pull the door behind him—but he didn't close it shut. I heard his steps as he walked slowly down the sidewalk to his car.

"Lord," I cried, "why do I always have to make such hard choices? I don't want Jerry to go, but I can't marry him, either. Yet, I know things can't stay the way they are; it's not fair to him. Please help me!" That moment appeared frozen in time.

Finally, I heard God whisper to my mind, *You have trusted Me in the past in every difficult situation and I helped you. I will always help, but I won't make your decisions for you. You struggle with the decision to marry Jerry because fear holds you in bondage. I am stronger than fear, but it is your decision to reject the painful memories of the past that will set you free. Your trust in Me will then have room to grow.*

I ran to the door and threw it open. Jerry stood at the end of the walk, stoop-shouldered, with head bowed. "Please, don't go!" I called out. Jerry whirled around as I rushed up to him. Under the streetlight, I saw his eyes widen in hope. Throwing myself into his open arms, I exclaimed, "I will marry you!"

He held me for a moment, then pushed me away. His hands gripped my arms. "Are you sure?" he asked, voice cautious, eyes intent as they bore into mine.

The urgency of the situation prompted the truth from my heart as I answered without thinking, "Yes," I said, "I love you." But Jerry would not hear those words again until our honeymoon.

Ours wasn't a long engagement, for a month later we were married. Maybe it was because neither of us wanted to give me time to back out again. During the month's flurry of wedding preparations, I still couldn't tell Jerry I loved him. Though he didn't understand any more than I did why I couldn't say those words, he was patient. He knew I loved him even if I didn't know it. Besides, he too was trusting his heavenly Father.

After the wedding, however, and on our honeymoon, it was a different story. Because Jerry and I were now truly one, both loving and trusting our future to the same God, I relaxed. I constantly showered Jerry with kisses and repeated over and over, "I love you, I love you!" I said it so often it almost drove him crazy.

"Okay, okay," he said one day, laughing, "I know you love me!"

But I was making up for lost time.

~

Almost two years later, our son David was born. Four years later, after experiencing the heartbreak of three miscarriages, one resulting in a burial, we were finally blessed with our beautiful daughter, Tamara. Life was good and we were happy.

CUPID VISITS THE REST OF THE FAMILY

My sister Chris married and had children, and my brother Chuck married and had a family. After dating Ira, her supervisor at work, Mom announced their engagement. Ira was a handsome former Air Force pilot who possessed all of the qualities that our father lacked. Six months later, they married.

We were happy for Mom. We prayed that her marriage would derail her bitterness. Though Cupid's arrow was firm and straight, it could not penetrate the inner core of hate at the center of

Mom's heart. Her obsession over her past abuse by our father grew with each passing year. She felt betrayed by us children, who had each forgiven our father and released our past.

"How on earth could you forgive Clyde Crawley?" (Mom refused to refer to Dad as our father.) "Have you forgotten what he did to me? He tried to beat me to death with a claw hammer—remember!"

"I know, Mom," I often said, giving her a hug. "How could we ever forget something so terrible? We forgave Dad because we want to be free of him. You are still his prisoner because your hate keeps him in your thoughts day and night. You may as well still be with him."

No amount of reasoning from us children could convince mother of the wisdom of forgiveness. We redoubled our expressions of love to her and intensified our prayers in her behalf. Every irritant that Mom experienced in life, however, was blamed upon our father, who thankfully had not reappeared.

But the time was fast approaching when he would reenter the lives of his children.

Chapter Nine

God's Mysterious Ways

One day I met Joan Englander in our little town of Ojai, California, where we then lived. She was a reporter for a weekly column in our local newspaper. I realized later that God had directed our conversation, for she picked up on something I said and asked, "You have domestic abuse in your background?"

Surprised at her question, I nodded yes.

"How is that you are so loving, accepting, and outgoing when you come from a bad environment?"

"I never really thought about it. I guess it's because I'm a Christian," I stammered.

I rarely reflected on my past. I considered myself a positive person, and I believed my past was negative. Besides, I had forgiven my father and felt there was no need to think about my childhood, much less mention it. Most of my friends were unaware of my background, and

I saw no reason for them to know. I was surprised that I had said anything to Joan that alluded to it.

I wasn't aware of it at the time, but I still carried deep feelings of shame. As a young child, we had lived on "the other side of the tracks." We were considered by some to be "riffraff—white trash." My father's abuse of us merely confirmed those labels. I was afraid that if anyone learned about my background they would lose respect for me.

Feelings of guilt can be dealt with through forgiveness and release, but shame is not so easily addressed. It wraps itself subtly around our psyche and whispers that we are of less value than others. Silence about my painful childhood only fertilized my feelings of shame, which grew best in darkness, away from God's light of truth. When God brought Joan into my life, He set into motion a chain of events that freed me from my chains of shame and affected the events of my life thereafter.

Joan said she wanted to write a story for her column about my background of abuse and how I overcame it, but I was reluctant.

"Why would you want to write a story about me?"

"Because only God could have taken away your fear and replaced it with such powerful love. This is a miracle that has to be told! Statistics regarding abuse victims clearly show that your story isn't typical—it's out of the ordinary." I stared at her, without comprehension

"Most individuals who suffer abuse grow up to either marry someone who abuses them, or they abuse their spouse and children, they take drugs or alcohol, or become victims of prostitution. And when they have children, the process starts all over again. You see, abuse is a vicious cycle that is often carried from generation to generation. But you beat the odds! The world needs to know what God has done in your life."

Statistics had always impressed me, so I gave her request serious consideration. After struggling with the idea, I talked it over with Jerry, and we prayed about it. Maybe deep inside I hoped he would be against it, but he said, "Whatever you feel led to do, honey. It's your choice."

At last, I fearfully consented to a story, but I asked to remain anonymous.

"That's not possible," Joan explained. "I only do personal interviews." So I again relented. Midway through the interview, Joan stopped taking notes and looked at me, visibly moved. Tears slipped from her eyes as she said, "God is going to use this story to touch countless lives!"

I had no doubt that God would use Joan's article, for by this time I was convinced that was why she and I had met.

Following the interview, Joan said she needed an accompanying photo for the article. I balked. I had hoped that only a few people would read my story, but with my picture included, everyone I knew would see it and be sure to read the article.

"Why do you want a picture?" I groaned.

"Because you don't look like the typical victim. There is a glow, a radiance about you that the world needs to see."

Though I didn't understand the point she labored to make, I finally relented. But I was nervous. I prayed, "Lord, I know You are orchestrating all of this. So please help me to overcome my feelings of shame and not be afraid of what people might think. Help me to trust You to use my story any way You want."

Meanwhile, Joan worried. Titles for her articles were selected by one of the editors, and she felt they might use something too sensational. She waited anxiously for the first press run.

A short while later, a subdued Joan appeared at my door with several newspaper copies. "I just hope," she said, chewing her lip, "that you're not offended by the title. I was afraid this might happen," she said, shaking her head.

I flipped the paper over to the back page to her column. At first I was shocked by the bold title glaring at me from the page. Then I was struck by the sudden realization that although

Joan had no control over the title selection, God did. And He had a sense of humor! I laughed and said, "The title is perfect."

When I later showed the article to Jerry, however, he saw no humor in its title. He was angry. "Everyone is going to think I abuse you!"

"But not for long," I said, laughing. "It's obvious that God wants exposure for His power through this article, and He's going to get it!"

Holding the paper up again for Jerry to see, I pointed to the offensive headline and exclaimed, "There is not one person in this entire small valley who will see my picture below this title and not read every word—"Battered Woman Tells Story." And I was right.

Everyone I knew was stunned by the article. The reaction of our dear friend Ferd Sobol was typical. With eyes crinkled in humor and voice tinged in admiration, he took my hands, looked into my eyes, and said, "Kitty, Kitty, Kitty—I had no idea you came from such a rough background. I always thought of you as just a sweet and smiling, pretty, plastic lady who was born with a silver spoon in her mouth. But you are one tough lady with real substance! I am impressed."

I was not offended by his candor. I cherished his response, for it was graphic evidence that God knew what He was doing. This article showed the truth of God's power in a person's life. And with an added benefit for me—I was no longer ashamed.

After reading that story, my friend Gerry King, who was an area representative for Stonecroft Ministries, invited me to a speaker's workshop in Ventura, California. From there I became a speaker at Christian Women's Club Luncheons and After-Five Dinner meetings, where for over twenty-five years I have told countless women the good news that they, too, can become overcomers.

Several years later, following a luncheon one day, an attractive young woman approached me with a question. "Have you seen your father since his release from prison?"

"No," I answered.

"Then how do you know you have really forgiven him? You might feel differently if you were to see him again."

I believed I had forgiven Dad, but I wasn't sure how I would feel if I saw him again face to face. The validity of my forgiveness would be tested only one year later.

THE TEST

We hadn't seen Dad in thirty years when he contacted my brother Chuck. Dad was remarried and had a married son. We were surprised to learn that our father and his wife, Marie, lived in our same state. After great deliberation, Chuck and his wife Nancy took their family to visit Dad and Marie. Following that visit, Dad began corresponding with Chris and me, begging us to also visit him. But we were reluctant.

"Do you think we can trust him?" Chris asked.

"I don't know," I said, shaking my head. "In his letters he swears that he has changed. But I'd love to know how he's been treating his second family."

"I'm not sure I want to know," Chris said shivering. "Chuck wasn't too sure, either," she added. "Remember? When he visited Dad the first time, he went alone to check things out before taking his family."

"Well, Dad hasn't bothered us all of these years, so maybe he has changed," I said hopefully.

At Dad's insistence, we finally agreed to visit him. One Saturday morning, Jerry and I, with Chris and her husband Everett, made the three-hour drive to Dad's home in Southern California. We rang the doorbell and waited. My pulse raced and I reached for Chris's hand. It was sweaty, as was mine.

Dad opened the door, flashed us a nervous smile, and hesitated for a moment. His cold blue eyes, now a little paler, darted from Chris to me.

He looked the same, only older. He was still very trim, but his sandy-brown hair appeared dyed and his face looked as though it had recently undergone a chemical peel.

He seems shorter! I thought. *Somehow his 5' 6" height had appeared much taller when we were children and he loomed over us as a monster.*

Dad reached out and embraced us girls. We responded stiffly. He then shook hands vigorously with our husbands, who appeared instantly impressed by his winsome charm.

Dad introduced us to Marie, a tiny brunette only one year older than I. There was something strangely familiar about her, but I didn't know what. Sensing her apprehension, I ignored her extended hand and hugged her. She smiled in relief.

After retiring to the family room, Marie served coffee while Chris and I showed Dad pictures of his grandchildren, three for her and two for me. Dad's hands trembled as he pored over each photo. Later he brought out their family albums, photographic evidence of happy family outings.

I leaned back in the overstuffed chair and breathed in the sweet fragrance of orange blossoms cascading through the open window. I relaxed as I listened to the soft voices of the others deep in conversation.

I can't believe I'm really here, I mused. Suddenly, the significance of the moment hit me. *This has got to be a miracle—to sit here in the presence of the man I once hated and feared so much that I wanted him dead, yet I feel nothing but compassion and peace! This proves that my forgiveness is real. Thank You, Lord.*

From time to time, I sneaked peaks at Marie's face, trying to read her expressions, looking for telltale signs of abuse, but found none. I caught Chris doing the same, and when our eyes met, we shrugged slightly.

While the others visited, Marie invited me for a walk in their garden. I was glad for an opportunity to be alone with her. I soon discovered that Marie was a Christian, was active in her church, sang in the choir, and obviously loved the Lord. She was a sweet, trusting soul who knew only what Dad had chosen to tell her of his past. As I listened to her gentle voice, I suddenly realized why she looked familiar. With her dark hair, deep green eyes, and cameo complexion, she bore a striking resemblance to my mother when she was Marie's age.

As we walked, Marie said, "Your dad has been a good husband to me and father to our son. He may be demanding and controlling sometimes, but he has never been physically abusive." She glanced at me but I said nothing. She continued, "Before we were married, he was honest with me about his past. He told me about his one mistake."

"One mistake?" I asked

"Yes. That time when he was sick and almost killed your mother." She hesitated, searching for the right words. "You know, because your mother was such a 'bad' woman."

A fiery anger flared within me. I wanted to lash out and burn this ignorant, trusting woman with the branding iron of truth. How dare she believe Dad's lies about my mother! But the Holy Spirit nudged me. *Why do you want to hurt her? She has done nothing wrong. She believes your father's lies just as your mother did.*

With great control, I said gently, "All I will say, Marie, is this: Our mother was a good wife and a wonderful mother."

Marie opened her mouth to reply, but held her response. Controlling her anger, she finally said, "Your father is very hurt because you children have ignored him all these years."

Now it was my turn to say nothing. We walked into the house in stiff, strained silence.

Chapter Ten

Had Our Father Really Changed?

Later, in the car on the way home, the four of us discussed whether or not we thought Dad had really changed. The guys felt sure he had, but we girls weren't convinced.

"I feel sorry for him," I said, "but I think he's the same con that he always was. I think he's just doing everything he can to snatch a little time with the children he once abused."

"I just don't know," Chris said. "But I'm inclined to agree with Kitty."

Our husbands argued in Dad's defense. "Then why hasn't he abused his second family all these years?" Everett asked.

"He took Marie and your half-brother on family outings and did lots of fun things with them.

"They certainly didn't look miserable and abused in their pictures," Jerry added.

"Neither did we!" I retorted.

"And he goes to church with Marie," Everett observed.

"Only rarely," I corrected, recalling Marie's and my conversation in the garden.

"But he helps out at the Forest Home Christian Campgrounds up in the mountains—even donated a station wagon to them. Remember how proud he was when he showed us pictures of it?"

"Besides, if he hasn't changed, how has he been able to hold his violent nature in check all these years?"

Their comments, tossed back and forth, echoed my own mental battle. I admitted I didn't have an answer. Only God knew.

~

The following spring, when Dad and Marie visited us in our Ojai home, Marie appeared withdrawn and pensive. When we were alone, she asked searching questions about Dad's past. She knew I sometimes gave away tapes of my Christian Women's Club speech, which covered my past abuse and forgiveness. She requested a tape, but I politely refused. She persisted.

"Why do you want this tape, Marie?"

She finally admitted, "I'm afraid of your dad. He is in the early stages of Parkinson's disease, and he is becoming obsessed with death. He fears gradually losing control of his life, and then dying." She hesitated, unsure of how to phrase her words. "He's making strange accusations. Although he has never hit me, I'm now afraid he will."

"What kind of accusations?" I probed. But she wouldn't elaborate.

Just before they left, I slipped her a tape and asked her to hide it. "Both of our lives will be in danger if Dad finds it," I warned. She nodded in agreement. From that tape she would learn at least part of the truth about Dad's past.

Several months later, Dad plunged their car off a cliff in the San Bernardino Mountains in a murder/suicide attempt. Marie was thrown clear, but halfway down, the car caught on a ledge. Dad suffered only minor injuries. While he was transported by helicopter to the nearest hospital, Marie described Dad's deliberate attempt to kill her and himself to the officers at the accident scene. Dad was put under house arrest and, following his hospital release, was jailed pending his hearing.

Marie called me frequently from a nearby pay phone during Dad's incarceration. "I think your father has our phone line bugged," she explained. "Besides, I don't want any record of my calls to you."

I told Marie everything about Dad's past, leaving nothing out. During one of our conversations, I asked, "Marie, what did you mean when you were at our house and said Dad had started 'accusing' you?"

"Your dad often accused me of having an affair—said he wouldn't tolerate another man enjoying his wife and possessions after his death."

My throat tightened and my heart pounded with realization. "Marie, you've got to leave! Dad accused my mom of the same thing before he tried to murder her."

Ignoring my statement, she continued, "Since he's been in jail, though, he's been nice. Says he didn't mean to go over the cliff. Said he just wasn't feeling well. I think psychiatric counseling will help," she said, hope in her voice.

"Marie, listen to me. In your garden you told me how devastated Dad was by his prison experience, and how he vowed he would never go to prison again. I now understand why he has held a leash on his violence all of these years. It isn't because he has changed, it's because he fears prison."

"No," she said loyally, "counseling will help. I can't believe he'd really want to hurt me."

"Marie," my voice shook, "he tried to kill you! That's why he's in jail, remember? He will try to kill you again, and the next time he will succeed! He'll use a gun—not a car."

"Then I'll just have to trust God," she said, sighing.

"We should always trust God, Marie, but He trusts us too—to use the common sense He gave us. You've got to leave!"

My efforts to persuade Marie of the danger she was in finally bore fruit, but to no avail. One morning, she called and filled me in on all that had happened since our last conversation. She said she had related to the judge everything I had told her, but her efforts to convince him that Dad was dangerous and should not be released were futile.

"Since your father has never physically abused me all of these years, the judge discounted everything you had told me about your dad's past."

"Excuse me!" I yelled. "You mean the fact that Dad was standing before him for attempted murder of you isn't evidence that he is violent?"

"I guess not," she said, sadness in her voice. With sudden crisp sarcasm, Marie added, "Your father's female attorney made a very convincing plea on his behalf! She said I was just paranoid because of all that you had told me, and that you had a personal vendetta against your father. She told the judge, 'Mr. Crawley's foot just slipped and he accidentally hit the gas pedal instead of the brake.' "

Marie's voice began to shake as she continued. "Then I spoke up again and reminded the judge how terrified I was at the lookout point. How, when Clyde got out of the car, he looked over the edge as if checking out the terrain below. He was assessing it, not admiring it! I related how nervous I was as I watched him. When your father got back into the car, I saw him deliberately put it into drive. Not R for reverse, but D for drive! I knew what he was going to do and I screamed out, 'No, Clyde, don't do this!' but it was too late. He jammed the gas pedal and we went flying over the cliff."

I shivered as I visualized the terrifying scene. "What did the judge say when you told him all of that?"

"Nothing; he just smiled. Ignoring what I said, he shuffled some papers and was quiet for a moment. He looked at your father and said, 'You are released on your own recognizance, pending your hearing.' He looked over at me and added, 'Now, Mr. Crawley, don't you go and hurt anyone,' and laughed."

White-hot anger flared within me at the ignorant judge. *How could he make such an insensitive, stupid remark!* My shoulders sagged as I fought an overwhelming sense of futility. *Marie is never going to make it. She doesn't have a chance—and it's so unfair!* But my fear for Marie refueled my efforts to help her.

"Marie, there is still time to leave. Let him get his own transportation from jail. Let his cute attorney drive him home," I snapped. "But you—you should pack and leave. Immediately!"

"I can't. I've done all I can," she said, her voice edged in fear. "Besides, where would I go? If I went to my mom's house, or any other relative, he would just find me, and their lives would be in danger. But," she added, a false note of hope in her voice, "I really think everything will be okay. Thank you for everything, Kitty. I've got to leave now and pick him up."

"Please call me when you get a chance," I begged. "I need to know what is happening."

"If I can, I will," she promised.

Hot tears burned my skin as they trickled down my face. "I will pray for you, Marie, and I'll pray for Dad—that he will listen to God's voice and not do what I'm afraid he will do."

That was the last time we spoke.

Six weeks later, when my father failed to appear at his hearing, two deputy sheriffs were dispatched to Dad's home to arrest him. There they found the bodies of Dad and Marie—dead from gunshot wounds.

WHY, GOD?

So there I sat at their funeral. My heavy heart again was tempted to ask, *Why, Lord?* But it remained quiet. It knew the answer.

I thought back to the previous day, when Chris and I sat at my kitchen table in Ojai discussing plans for our long drive to the funeral. Visibly shaken, Chris had run out of words and sat mute. I patted her hand and said, "We will get through this. The Lord will hold us close to Him and give us the strength we need. We just need to keep praying."

Chris remained silent. Taking a leisurely sip of coffee, she stared out the window. Large orange leaves floated gently downward as the huge old oak began an early shedding of its splashy autumn attire.

Chris turned her head slowly back to me. Fixing her sad brown eyes upon mine, she asked through trembling lips, "How can you still believe in prayer? I prayed and prayed. I begged God to speak to Dad and change his heart, and look what happened. What good does prayer do, anyway?"

It was my turn to gaze out the window, but only for a moment. There was no need for me to seek that which I had already discovered. Taking her hand in mine, I said, "I believe in prayer now more strongly than ever. I, too, prayed for Dad—that God would send the Holy Spirit to him and remind him of his need to accept Christ, to let go of his stubborn will, and to give God the broken pieces of his life to mend as only God can."

"And what good did it do? He didn't answer your prayers either," Chris said softly through gritted teeth. Tears of disappointment pooled in her eyes, threatening to spill.

"But He did. God heard all of our prayers."

"How can you say that?" she gasped in disbelief. "It's obvious He didn't answer them."

"Chris, we can't ask God to do something that will violate His integrity. He gave each of us a free will, which means we are not robots. We can make any choice we want. Though each of us will stand before God someday and be held accountable for those choices, He will never force any of us to do anything. That includes our father."

"So how, then, do you think God answered our prayers?"

"Think about it. Why would Dad wait six long, miserable weeks to do what he planned to do all along? It must have been difficult for him, hiding in their house behind closed doors, afraid to venture out because of the neighbors' stares and whispers, having to think up plausible answers to any close friend who might ask questions. He could have gone home and immediately done what he ultimately did. There was nothing to stop him. Why did he wait?"

Puzzled, but eager for my explanation, Chris shrugged.

"I believe Dad waited *because* of our prayers. It was during those long weeks that we were praying and asking God to send His Holy Spirit to speak to Dad. I believe it was during that time that the Holy Spirit tried to convince Dad that despite every wrong choice he had made in life, despite all of the heartaches and pain he had caused, not only others, but himself, God still loved him. I believe the Holy Spirit reminded Dad that Jesus had already paid for all of his sins on the cross—all he had to do was repent and ask forgiveness. I'm sure Dad understood the Holy Spirit's reasoning, for he wasn't ignorant of the Scripture. He had heard God's truth countless times throughout his life. It was that truth that he struggled against day after day until he ultimately made his choice."

Yesterday's conversation seemed so long ago.

I glanced again at the stark and bare casket with its single rose. *Oh Dad, why did you struggle so? Why didn't you just yield to God's love?*

~

We all struggle with our choices. Our wrong choices are powerful vehicles that can propel us, at high speeds, headlong in the wrong direction until we crash into the immovable wall of consequences. As we careen from one bad choice to another, however, not only do we suffer, but innocent people around us also suffer.

I'm sure my father didn't always deliberately set out to choose evil. But most of his choices were based upon expediency, selfishness, and his obsessive desire to control. Dad embraced whatever choice seemed to promise the results he sought. However, only God knows the havoc Dad could have wrought had he succumbed to all of his wrong inclinations. This is true of each of us.

How ironic that I, too, had struggled long ago with this same loving God when I thought the death of my father was my only way out. But because I made the right choice at that time, decades later I was able to pray for that same father who thought death was his only way out. My choice resulted in a new beginning for me. Dad's choice resulted in a tragic ending.

Because my choice led to life and not death, it opened the door for me to make another good choice, one that affects my current situation in dynamic proportions. That was the decision to forgive my father.

Had I not already forgiven Dad for his past wrongs, this current tragedy would revive my burning embers of resentment. I would relive in vivid detail all of the horrors of my father's past violence, particularly his gruesome attack on our mother. I would become even more enraged, with yet another layer of anger wound bitterly around my soul. I would have sat at the funeral out of stoic loyalty to Marie, hating my father, glaring grim-faced and tight-lipped at the two caskets. I would have shaken my fists mentally toward heaven, demanding an answer to "Why, God?"

Instead, I sat in the midst of a double tragedy, not as a bedraggled, hate-filled survivor, but as a victorious over-comer overwhelmed with God's sweet peace. I grieved over the tragic loss of Marie but rejoiced in the knowledge that she was in heaven.

I felt compassion for my father, and a bone-chilling sadness. I knew why this happened. Despite a lifetime of opportunities to make the right choice by yielding his life to a loving God, Dad had once again made the wrong choice—his final wrong choice.

~

What about you? Does your heart still struggle with bitterness and pain from the tragic effects flung upon you by the wrong choices made by others? Is there any hope that you can overcome your heartbreak and rise above it? Take courage—the answer is yes!

But how?

Part Two

CHAPTER ELEVEN

Changing My Self-Image

I was fascinated one day by a bumper sticker on the car ahead of me. It consisted of one question: "Who do you think you are?"

Our identity is often wrapped so tightly in our packaging—our passions, professions, or titles—that we rarely peel away the layers and discover who we really are. Consequently, many of us experience an identity crisis when we suddenly lose what we feel makes up our identity.

A number of years ago, a friend of mine was the wife of a successful, well-known surgeon. Without warning, her husband of many years divorced her. Heartbroken, she confided to me, "I don't know who I am anymore. I've always been known as Angela, Dr. Brown's wife."

THE POLICE WOMAN

Let me tell you about my friend, Carol.

Twenty-six-year-old police officer Carol Holdinsky called into her radio, "3 PAUL 14, in pursuit of a 211 suspect, W/M 6 ft., 160, wearing jean jacket and Levi's, S/B across Cypress Park. Request backup to arrest additional suspect near park entrance, roll rescue for robbery victim near his vehicle, white '78 Buick 4-door."

Carol, a former university track team runner still in excellent physical condition, sprinted after the suspect. When he scaled a six-foot wall ahead of her, she followed. Her eyes were glued on the suspect, and she didn't notice the asphalt drainage ditch below, angling toward the wall four feet lower than the ground. She landed full weight on her left leg, hyperextending and jamming her knee. The pain was excruciating, but the sudden rush of adrenaline propelled her on until she caught the suspect.

That accident resulted in five open-knee surgeries, each requiring nearly a year's recovery period, and forced Carol's early retirement at the age of thirty-six from a career she loved dearly. Before her retirement, she had undergone three additional knee surgeries, lost a baby due to deep vein thrombosis (a condition resulting from her injury), and gone through a divorce.

Carol and I became friends after meeting at a women's retreat. She sometimes accompanied me on out-of-town speaking trips, where I slowly learned her story.

"I've never heard you complain once about all of your painful surgeries, Carol. Aren't you bitter, even a little?"

"I've never been angry or bitter—not toward the suspect, it wasn't his fault, and not toward my circumstances. I was just doing my job. A job that I loved," she added sadly. Always interested in how people evolve into overcomers, I prodded, "You must have been angry at some time."

"Yes—but not over this incident. When I was 19 and in college, my dream was to become a world-class track athlete. I was good enough and my future looked bright. But one day, during the last practice before my first collegiate basketball game, I tore two ligaments in my left leg. This required hospitalization and extensive long-term physical therapy.

"I worked hard during physical therapy sessions, confident that I would recover and still accomplish my dream. But when the doctors told me I would never play again at my prior level, I was devastated.

"I recovered, but my dream didn't. Worse yet, not only was my athletic career ended, but I was forced to drop out of college—with only nine credit hours to go. Between rehab and lack of finances, I had neither the time nor the money to finish college. I was very angry!

"The sudden loss of my dreams threw me into an identity crisis. I had pictured myself as a college graduate and a world-class athlete. What would I do? It took a while, but I finally yielded to the Lord and let go of my bitterness. God helped me through that difficult time. But I suffered another identity crisis following my second accident.

"I had worked hard to become a police officer, and I saw myself functioning happily in that career until retirement. When I faced the possibility of a forced disability retirement at such a young age, I didn't know how to see myself. Who would I be if I couldn't function as a police officer?

"I spent hours talking with my second husband, John, who was also a police officer and a devout Christian. I mentioned the irony of how two different accidents to the same knee had permanently blocked two different directions that I thought my life was going. I was disoriented, just as I had been following my first accident. I was confused, but thank God, not angry and rebellious. I had grown beyond that.

"John helped me so much. 'Carol,' he said, 'being a police officer is not who you are—it is just what you do. You are identified as a police officer, but that is not your identity. First and foremost, you are a Christian. And wherever God puts you, you will be successful. Not because of your classification or title, but because of who you are—a child of God, called to follow Him regardless of where He leads.'

"I was glad that John had reminded me of what I knew, deep in my heart, was true. And actually, I wasn't aware of my lack of bitterness until you mentioned it. We learn based on our past experiences and prior training. My training comes from the discipline and self-control taught in God's Word. When I lost my baby, my husband, my career, and temporarily my identity, I could handle it because I knew Who was in control. Not I, not circumstances, but my heavenly Father."

Carol currently teaches classes in various churches on stress-related issues—between surgeries. Due to extended crutch and cane use, the rotator cuff in each shoulder was torn, requiring four more surgeries, three on one shoulder. To date, Carol has endured fourteen surgeries, two of which were total knee replacements on the same knee.

Due to her past and present circumstances of pain, Carol could have chosen the identity of a victim and lived out her life as a bitter survivor. But with God's help, she sees herself as she really is—a trusting daughter of the King. How do others see her? As a vivacious overcomer.

It has been said that the greatest psychological discovery of the twentieth century was the discovery of self-image. Each of us has a mental picture of who we are and what we are like. This image is built by our beliefs about ourselves and is our picture as to the sort of person we are.

As children, the picture we hold of ourselves is influenced greatly by the bold brush strokes of our environment. Strong feelings, good and bad, are the strokes used to paint our self-portrait. These feelings are referred to as "truth."

IS THE PICTURE CORRECT?

Too often our picture of who we think we are is painted by someone else. My father told me I was ugly and stupid. I don't know if he believed that or not, but those were his words. I could have either accepted them as truth or rejected them as merely his opinion. Children, however, are incapable of objectively evaluating statements made to them by others, especially adults. Because these words were spoken by an adult authority figure, my own father, I embraced them as truth. *Why would my father tell me I was ugly and stupid if it weren't so?* I reasoned. His abuse made me feel inferior, and consequently my feelings validated his negative descriptions of me—which led me to accept them as the truth. My young mind reasoned that no one would deliberately mistreat something of value, so I grew up believing I was worthless.

Because my mind accepted this incorrect picture, painted by someone else (someone in authority), I tried to "prove" the image I held of myself. In other words, I subconsciously tried to live up (or down) to that mental picture. My misconceptions were not unique to my situation. Each of us is affected by what others think and say about us.

In Zig Ziglar's book *See You at the Top*, he writes about a fifteen-year-old boy whose teacher told him he should drop out of school and learn a trade, because he lacked the intelligence to graduate from high school. Victor Seribriakoff took her advice. He became an itinerant worker doing a variety of jobs for the next seventeen years. At age thirty-two, however, Victor discovered that he was not a "dunce" as he had believed all those years. An evaluation revealed him to be a genius with an IQ of 161.

Armed with that new startling information, Victor gained newfound confidence. He began to accumulate knowledge, expecting and achieving different results. He became more effective and productive, until years later he had written numerous books, secured a number of patents, and become a successful businessman.

The most amazing accomplishment of this former high school dropout was his election as chairman of the International Mensa Society—which has only one membership qualification—an IQ of 140. When Victor saw himself differently, he started acting differently.

WHAT HAPPENS IF I DON'T CORRECT MY PICTURE?

I recall a line from a television sitcom that caused everyone to laugh, including me. One of the characters said, "Life is hard..." He then hesitated. Every body movement and facial expression let us know there was more to come. We waited for the expected words of wisdom, some helpful hints of hope—for each of us, deep in the heart of experience already knows that life, at times, is hard.

I held my breath in anticipation. He finally spoke and said, "...and then you die."

In the context of the script it was funny, for it was totally opposite of what we expected. Yet many people function within that sad picture of life, and it's not funny.

Unfortunately, because of the incorrect pictures we carry, many of us experience death before we die. Our hope for happiness crumbles into dust and lies at our feet. Faith that our future will differ from our past dwindles and dies. We are bone-weary, tired of trying because we are always disappointed. We even tire of the anger that once propelled us. We just don't care anymore, and we give up. We wait for death, but for all intents and purposes, we are already dead.

But it can be different. Our future holds promises of unbelievable happiness, fulfillment, and joy—if we change our picture. How is that possible? By using the gift God has given us to make different choices, choices that are grounded in truth. Choices that will lead to life and not to death.

Think about it.

Do you carry a picture of yourself that is not true? Ideas that keep you in bondage physically, mentally, or spiritually?

If so, God has good news for you: "And you will know the truth, and the truth will set you free" (John 8:32).

THE TRUTH ABOUT ME

My search for truth had to begin with God's Word, which tells us that God is the author of truth. Every word of truth that has been spoken since the beginning of time originated with God. Even when His truth is mouthed by liars and fools and twisted by evil men to accomplish their goals, truth is still truth—and God is still its author.

We are in a position to be set free from the incorrect picture we hold of ourselves when we embrace this reality—that God exists and that He is the author of all truth. Centuries ago, the psalmist looked up and proclaimed: "Only fools say in their hearts, 'There is no God' " (Psalm 14:1).

We commonly describe a fool as one who is not in touch with reality. For years I had lived out of touch with reality regarding my value as a human being. Getting in touch with reality required my looking at God. As I looked at Him and began to see what He is like, I began to see myself as He sees me.

In reevaluating my thought patterns and belief system within this new frame of reference, I soon realized how fortunate I had been that fateful night when I attended church with my Uncle Paul and in desperation had looked up.

In the first chapter of the Bible, God tells us that we were created in His image. We are not gods by any stretch of the imagination, but we were created with some of the characteristics of our Creator in that we can reason, respond, create, and communicate ideas. The psalmist recognized this and marveled: "You made all the delicate, inner parts of my body and knit me together in my mother's womb. Thank you for making me so wonderfully complex! Your workmanship is marvelous—and how well I know it" (Psalm 139:13-14).

The truth is, we are wonderfully complex and we have unbelievable potential. Some Bible translations include the statement that we are "fearfully and wonderfully made." And, indeed, we are "fearfully made." Because God gave us the freedom to choose, that reality can be downright scary! We can make choices that will result in our becoming a bully instead of a blessing, a terrorist instead of a tycoon, or a menace to mankind instead of a miracle worker in the world of medicine.

"There is a path before each person that seems right, but it ends in death" (Proverbs 14:12). The good news is: God did not create us and then leave us to ourselves to stumble around helplessly. He knows the pain we will experience when we try to live our lives without Him. We are vulnerable and inclined to make wrong choices. In the midst of certain circumstances, many otherwise decent people will kill, commit adultery, steal, and lie through bad choices, choices that will result in pain for everyone involved.

I came to realize that I could never become all I was created to be apart from the truths recorded in God's operator's manual, the Holy Bible. However, the Bible is more than a mere operation manual; it is God's love letter to us. Book by book, chapter by chapter, verse by verse, He pours out His miraculous love to each of us.

> Do not be afraid, for I have ransomed you. I have called you by name; you are mine. When you go through deep waters and great trouble. I will be with you. When you go through rivers of difficulty, you will not drown! When you walk through the fire of oppression, you will not be burned up; the flames will not consume you. For I am the Lord, your God...your Savior... you are precious to me. You are honored, and I love you (Isaiah 43:1-4).

God makes it possible for us to have a new identity through Christ. It matters not what we were like in the past or what current misconceptions we hold of ourselves. With God we can have an entirely new beginning.

"...It is by his boundless mercy that God has given us the privilege of being born again. Now we live with a wonderful expectation because Jesus Christ rose again from the dead" (1 Peter 1:3).

God wants us to choose Him, to choose the right ways for our lives. " 'For I know the plans

I have for you,' says the LORD. 'They are plans for good and not for disaster, to give you a future and a hope' " (Jeremiah 29:11).

I chose a new beginning with God at the age of fourteen. That new road led me away from the path of destruction to an avenue of wonderful possibilities as an overcomer.

WE NEED A SAVIOR

God knows that it is impossible for us to live rightly apart from Him. So He not only gave us His Word, He sent part of Himself—Christ the Savior—that we might have access to His love, power, and divine protection. It is only through Christ that we can reach God. And rightly so. Christ loved us enough to willingly leave all the beauty, wealth, and security of the heavenly kingdom to come to earth and suffer the agony and humiliation of death on the cross to pay for our sins. Because of His resurrection, the power of death was defeated and we have access to eternal life. Who else loves us that much? Talk about a Savior!

God also sent the Holy Spirit, our comforter and sustainer, who comes to dwell within us the moment we trust Christ. Through Him we have access to all the power and strength we need. What an opportunity! When we accept Christ into our lives, we get three for one—God the Father, Christ the Son, and the Holy Spirit. Talk about love!

When we accept Christ and all of His resurrected power into our lives, God gives us a new identity and a new reason for living. Talk about a new beginning!

"You must be...careful to put into action God's saving work in your lives, obeying God with deep reverence and fear" (Philippians 2:12).

This verse admonishes us to let the salvation experience that God performed on the inside work its way out into our daily living. A new identity will best be evidenced through outward actions. There is an old saying, "Talk is cheap." It is one thing to claim to be changed and another to live a life that reflects that change.

God will change our soul and give us a new identity, just as He did for me the night I trusted my life to Him through Christ. But there is one thing God will not do for us: He will not build our character. That is our responsibility. But how do we accomplish this? Where do we even begin?

Chapter Twelve

God Gives Life, We Build Character

> What we are is God's gift to us. What we become is our gift to God.
>
> – Anonymous writer as quoted by Eleanor Powell

Working on our gift to God must begin with accountability. This begins with the realization that we alone are responsible for building our personal character. No easy task. Will God help us? Of course! But it is through the daily choices we make that character is built. "...Choose today whom you will serve...But as for me and my family, we will serve the Lord" (Joshua 24:15).

Our character reflects our choices. What does the word "character" mean? Webster's defines it as "moral excellence and firmness." Our nation was founded by God-fearing men and women who proclaimed the importance of character. Its foundation was built on the principles outlined in God's Word that call for personal accountability—first to God, then to people.

People in the U.S. enjoy a great number of freedoms. But with freedom comes responsibility. Many of us clamor for more rights, but what we really seek is more license. We have enough freedom; what we really need is more accountability.

> Freedom is in danger of degenerating into mere arbitrariness unless it is lived in terms of responsibleness. That is why I recommend that the Statue of Liberty on the East Coast be supplemented by a Statue of Responsibility on the West Coast.
>
> —Viktor Frankl,
> *Man's Search for Meaning*

The ideal of character has suffered blows in recent years. Too many people, from the highest levels of society down to the average mom and dad, have displayed an abysmal lack of character. Sadly, we see little difference between the lifestyles of many Christians and non-Christians. The divorce rate is the same. More and more Christian women become unwed mothers. Some Christian women also kill their unborn babies. Many couples, young and old alike, who call themselves Christians live together outside of marriage. The young say it is cheaper than marrying since there are no legal fees when they split up. The old claim financial benefits because they don't have to give up their pensions. If character costs us any type of inconvenience, it seems, Christian or not, we dump it.

VICTIMS OF OUR ENVIRONMENT?

Society tells us that we are helpless creatures of our circumstances—captive victims of our past. We are led to believe that our thoughts and actions, which originated from early childhood experiences and lie deeply buried in our subconscious mind, can never be understood, and will forever control us. How depressing! No wonder millions seek counseling as their savior. If I accepted these theories as fact and did not believe the Bible, I would be first in line!

Unfortunately, many in today's society who believe we are victims of our environment consequently believe that we should not be held responsible for our actions. But what about reason and choice?

When God created us, He gave us a powerful gift: a free will to reason and choose that sets us apart from the rest of His creation. There are those who would have us believe that difficult circumstances can overpower our gift of reason, leaving us no choice but to live as animals. Thus, heinous atrocities are committed by individuals who claim no responsibility.

Mothers kill their babies and blame PMS, postpartum blues, or "hard times." Men rape and kill any gender they can get their hands on and blame their parents for not loving them as children. Millions of unborn babies are aborted because their entrance into this world would cause inconvenience. Students kill fellow classmates because they feel rejection. Ex--employees go on shooting sprees because they were fired.

And so it goes—a sad commentary of our time in which no one is responsible for anything. And this takes place in one of the most civilized countries on earth—a nation that is rapidly becoming uncivilized.

If we disobey God's commandments and break man's laws, are we not to be held accountable? If we are not responsible for our actions because of our environment, neither are our parents, nor theirs, nor anyone else who lives or has ever lived. If our nation continues down this road of "no-fault" crimes, how are we different from animals? Would we not then live in a "survival of the fittest" or "kill or be killed" animalistic world?

Sadly, the guilty and innocent alike suffer from this attitude. Year after year, psychiatrist offices and self-help groups are filled to capacity with hurting individuals who blame someone else for their ongoing discomfort.

Our first and most important step in the building of character is to assume responsibility for our actions. Responsibility, however, is more than mere acknowledgment of one's wrong behavior. Our prisons are full of people who admit their crimes, but they blame someone else. In his book *A Nation of Victims*, Author Charles J. Sykes points out:

> Paradoxically, this don't-blame-me permissiveness is applied only to the self, not to others; it is compatible with an ideological Puritanism that is notable for its shrill demands of psychological, political, and linguistic correctness. The ethos of victimization has an endless capacity not only for exculpating one's self from blame, washing away responsibility in a torrent of explanation—racism, sexism, rotten parents, addiction, and illness—but also for projecting guilt onto others.

THERE IS HOPE

Despite our rebellion, God showed His abiding love by promising to send an antidote for this terminal spiritual disease called sin. The antidote? His Son, Jesus Christ— the Messiah. And what better way for our Savior to become acquainted with our humanness, our frailties, our pain, and our temptations than to become flesh and dwell among us?

He came knowing that He would pay dearly for His trip. But He had to come. He knew we would all perish without a spiritual transfusion. Only His pure, untainted blood, transfused via the cross, could provide an acceptable antidote for sin.

There is hope. All across our nation, there are positive steps being taken to promote the importance of building character in today's youth. In the December 2001 issue of our local independent newspaper in Gilbert, Arizona, we read the following:

> **Community With Character—**The Gilbert Community With Character Committee, a nonprofit volunteer group promoting character education programs throughout the community, recently launched its campaign to promote six "pillars of character."
>
> Gilbert has been designated a Community With Character since 2000, when the Gilbert Town Council, Chamber of Commerce Board of Directors and Gilbert

> Public Schools Governing Board adopted resolutions.
>
> Since then, the Community With Character Committee has been organizing programs in a variety of areas to promote character traits. The six pillars they have chosen are Responsibility, Trustworthiness, Citizenship, Caring, Fairness and Respect. One pillar will be highlighted each month.
>
> The Committee has been divided into six sectors, focusing on the following areas:
>
> **School Sector**—The Gilbert Public School District has received a $400,000 federal grant to implement character education into each of its schools. More than 40 teachers have attended training and have begun incorporating the character traits into classroom discussions.

The other five sectors listed were Town Government Sector, Business Sector, Faith Community Sector, Family Sector, and Non-Profit Sector, with a brief description of character-building plans for each. The article concluded: "If you'd like to learn more about the Community With Character program, visit their website at www.gilbertcharacter.com."

It is noteworthy that the first character attribute listed in this article is responsibility. But before we can act responsibly, we must first develop a proper attitude. It is easy to fall into the "it's not my fault" victim mentality and look for someone else to blame. It is especially important for those of us who have been victims to assume responsibility for our actions and resist the temptation to make excuses for our wrong choices.

There are times, of course, when blame-placing thoughts are appropriate. As a helpless child I blamed my father for my unhappiness, and he *was* the cause of my heartaches. But as I grew in years and maturity, I began to understand that though my father was the cause of most of my problems when I was young, he was not responsible for *every* heartache I would experience for the rest of my life. Nor was it fair to blame him for discomforts that come with living in an imperfect world. Charles Sykes continues:

> Increasingly, Americans act as if they had received a lifelong indemnification from misfortune and a contractual release from personal responsibility. The British Economist noted with bemusement that in the United States, "If you lose your job you can sue for the mental distress of being fired. If your bank goes

> broke, the government has insured your deposits...If you drive drunk and crash you can sue somebody for failing to warn you to stop drinking. There is always somebody else to blame."
>
> Unfortunately, that is a formula for social gridlock: the irresistible search for someone or something to blame colliding with the unmovable unwillingness to accept responsibility.
>
> —Charles J. Sykes, *A Nation of Victims*

God's Word has much to say about responsibility. God gives clear-cut personal, family, and social guidelines that call for self-discipline and accountability. And He offers wisdom.

> If you need wisdom—if you want to know what God wants you to do—ask him, and he will gladly tell you. He will not resent you asking. But when you ask him, be sure that you really expect him to answer, for a doubtful mind is as unsettled as a wave of the sea that is driven and tossed by the wind. People like that should not expect to receive anything from the Lord. They can't make up their minds. They waver back and forth in everything they do...Whatever is good and perfect comes to us from God above who

> created all heaven's lights. Unlike the wind, he never changes or casts shifting shadows. In his goodness he chose to make us his own children by giving us his true word. And we, out of all creation, became his choice possession (James 1:5-8, 3:17-18).

But what about the bitterness and pain we feel when we are hurt by those who choose not to live by God's guidelines? Surely we can't be held responsible for those feelings. Despite how we may feel, we are responsible for dealing appropriately with our hurts.

> Don't copy the behavior and customs of this world, but let God transform you into a new person by changing the way you think. Then you will know what God wants you to do, and you will know how good and pleasing and perfect his will really is (Romans 12:2).

What is the pattern of the world? "I don't get mad—I get even." "Payback time!" "Make my day!" God says we are not to respond as the world does. Through the assimilation and practice of God's words and the prompting of other Christians, I was able to forgive my father and get on with my life. I am emotionally healed.

I live a productive life today, unshackled by neuroses and free of bitterness.

Some may call me simplistic, but I believe our problems would be solved if we read the Bible, believed it, and sought the aid of the Holy Spirit to incorporate God's counsel into our lives. But most of us don't. That's why so many of us seek earthly counselors. Earthly counselors can help us with some problems, but only God can truly heal a life.

Of course there are times when I struggle, argue, and balk at some of God's instructions. But I ultimately end up trusting His counsel. After all, He made me! The more accountable I am to God, the more I believe and test the truth of His words, and the more evidence I accumulate that they are true. Then I trust God even more—a beautiful spiritual cycle that builds character from the inside out.

Chapter Thirteen

A Mighty Counselor

I once worked part-time with a Christian woman who frequented her psychiatrist's couch. As a child she had experienced sexual fondling by an uncle, and was now heavy into therapy. During our breaks we had opportunity to get better acquainted. She appeared to be trapped in a time warp of victimization, unable to get beyond her childhood experience.

I asked if she had forgiven her uncle. She said "yes," but her anger was apparent when she spoke of him. I gave her a tape of one of my speeches, hoping my experiences might help her. She returned it without comment, but I soon sensed her disapproval.

During one of our breaks one day, she announced with raised brows, "You are in denial about your pain. You put on the appearance of being healed and carefree, but you have never dealt with your terrible past. That's why you give speeches, laugh, and cut up so much. It's all a front. No one can come through what you did without professional help. You need serious counseling."

I understood her assumption. I had met people who were in denial, afraid to face the cause of their suppressed pain, living behind a facade. But they were survivors, not overcomers. I knew the difference.

"Jane, how do you think God has managed to help His children for over 2,000 years without the aid of professional counselors? Has He just been fumbling along, drumming His fingers, waiting patiently for professionally trained counselors to come to His rescue? God's power is not limited. Don't you believe God when He says that His Word is sharper and more powerful than any two-edged sword? And that belief, acceptance, and adherence to His Word can change lives? Despite what you think, God has helped me to become an overcomer—and without the aid of professional counselors."

She studied me through her dark-rimmed glasses and opened her mouth, ready for rebuttal.

Not yet ready to give ground, I continued. "I would be presumptuous if I said that because I was healed without the aid of professional counseling, it is not necessary for you or anyone else to seek counseling. It is likewise presumptuous for you to say that it is impossible for me, or anyone else, to be healed *without* professional counseling."

She closed her mouth, and without response we returned to our desks in silence.

Why is it that we can wholeheartedly accept the Scriptures that proclaim God's ability to love a sinful, despicable person, forgive him, give him a new heart and purpose in life, prepare for him a beautiful place in eternity, and yet balk at Scriptures that promise His children the wisdom to overcome the negative actions of others? Does that sound reasonable—that Christ would die for the sinner and make all these wonderful accommodations for him and then neglect him when he suffers hurt after becoming a Christian?

In Jane's defense, she had simply bought into the prevailing attitude of the time that without lengthy counseling all victims were doomed to a life of misery and dysfunction. She had also succumbed to the incorrect idea that "every family is dysfunctional and needs counseling."

VOLUNTEER VICTIMS?

Of course, unkind words directed toward us hurt our feelings. But many individuals, who have no idea what it is to suffer real physical, mental, and emotional terror at the hands of a predator, eagerly rush to the counselor's couch and volunteer to be victims. They give hard-earned money (theirs or someone else's) to counselors who dig deeply into their past to unearth some form of abuse that would provide some reason for their dysfunctions, neuroses, anxieties, anger, or low self-esteem. After all, their problems must be the fault of someone else!

Why would anyone *want* to be labeled a victim? Could it be that as a victim we feel we can avoid making hard and practical choices to assume responsibility for our own faulty thinking and actions? And yet, in all fairness, maybe many of us just don't know how.

MY WONDERFUL COUNSELOR

I didn't know how to solve my problems; I wasn't even sure what they were. All I knew was that I was miserable. But when I went to my wonderful Counselor and listened to Him, my attitude began to change. This opened the door to healing. Who is my counselor?

> For a child is born to us, a son is given to us. And the government will rest on his shoulders. These will be his royal titles: Wonderful Counselor, Mighty God, Everlasting Father, Prince of Peace (Isaiah 9:6).

My emotional healing took place not on a counselor's couch but on my knees before the throne of the mighty God—aka wonderful Counselor. Openly and honestly, I bowed in pain before Him. In love, He listened as I daily vented my frustrations. He was patient as I questioned the wisdom of His counsel recorded in the Bible regarding anger: "And don't sin by letting anger gain control over you. Don't let the sun go down while you are still angry, for anger gives a mighty foothold to the devil. Get rid of all bitterness, rage, anger, harsh words, and slander, as well as all types of malicious behavior" (Ephesians 4:26-27,31).

God understood when I questioned the practicality of forgiveness. He held my heart together as I cried and debated the logic of praying for some-one who was hurting me. He then blew His breath of love deep into my soul where He saw a tiny glowing desire to obey Him, and fanned it into a burning flame of desire to closely follow His instructions.

My most important step in healing was the giving up of all rights to myself. I let go of my "right" to hate and seek revenge, to wallow in pain and self-pity. When I gave up my "rights," I found freedom.

Though not received in a professional counselor's office, counseling has played a vital role in my healing and growth. Each time I listen with open mind to a sermon by a godly minister, I am counseled. Each Sunday school lesson, presented by a godly teacher and discussed by class members, stretches my growth. I glean counsel from each conversation with a person who "walks his talk."

And the impact made upon my life by God-inspired books, articles, audio tapes, videos, and Christian radio talk show programs can never be measured!

I believe one of the single most important aids in my becoming an overcomer is a love for truth—God's truth, not man's opinion of truth. Truth is reality. It is our flawed thinking, our warped perceptions that prevent us from recognizing reality.

> Truth exists; only falsehood has to be invented.
>
> —Georges Braque

Many survivors live in a subjective world of feelings that has little to do with reality. Only when we see ourselves and our circumstances correctly can we take the appropriate steps to become an overcomer.

"When the Spirit of truth comes, he will guide you into all truth..." (John 16:13). God is the author of truth, and the Holy Spirit leads me to its benefits. God's Word counseled me regarding what types of thoughts I should think. (Particularly helpful to me are the admonitions found in the fourth chapter of Philippians.)

Due to my negative background, I was starved for material promoting positive and inspirational thoughts that called for accountability. I gorged my mind on books and tapes written by authors such as Robert Schuller, Dale Carnegie, Zig Ziglar, Victor Frankl, Adrian Rogers, Chuck Swindoll, and Dr. James Dobson. Rich is the counsel found in the book *Telling Yourself the Truth* by William Backus and Marie Chapian, and Joyce Meyer's *The Battlefield of the Mind.*

So have I been helped by counseling? Yes. God's truths from all sources help mold my character.

COUNSELORS ARE NEEDED

Of course, there are times when professional counseling is helpful and needed! But we must be careful in our selection of a counselor. He or she should be a God-fearing person who uses God's principles skillfully. We can't assume that every professional counselor who claims to be spiritual is a competent counselor. Nor should we assume that just anyone with a degree in psychology can help in every situation. For example, children who have been violently sexually abused should be counseled by professionals trained in treating that specific type of abuse.

The responsible counselor will concern himself/herself more with how quickly and effectively you can be helped to assume personal responsibility for your emotional and mental health than with how long he can keep you digging in the pit of your past pains—and digging into your pockets for return trips.

It is fruitless to keep rehashing the past, year after year, with no real effort at moving beyond our pain, since that keeps our focus on our victimization. Neither does it do us any good to seek the wise counsel of godly counselors if we aren't willing to follow their advice. It must be frustrating for competent counselors to feel that, in some cases, they are merely high-priced emotional babysitters.

Undergirding everything we do to become overcomers must be a desire to put God first in our life; to absorb the truth of His words into our mind and soul and seek His guidance in everything.

Bad things happen to good people—that is reality. We must expect it, face it, deal with it, and overcome it. If we refuse to adjust to this reality, we can do far more damage to ourselves than could anyone else.

A PRISONER SET FREE

My friend Winnie relates this amazing story about her mother.

> The police took Mom away in restraints, kicking and screaming. Her years of silent hate for our father had finally erupted, carrying her to a dark place in her mind and holding her prisoner. She underwent twenty-five shock treatments in a psychiatric hospital, was released two months later on psychotropic drugs, and received twenty-five additional shock treatments as an outpatient.
>
> Despite treatment, Mom worsened. She spent her days sitting disheveled in a rocker, staring out the window of their home in a semi-catatonic state. I was a new Christian and begged God, "Please make my mom like she used to be."
>
> After praying for Mom for two years with no signs of improvement, I was discouraged to the point of quitting. "Lord, what can I do? Despite my prayers, there isn't even a small ray of hope that you will restore Mom to her former self."
>
> I heard God's still small voice say, "I won't return your mother to her former self, but when I am finished working with

her she will know Me in ways that she has never known Me."

The Lord impressed Psalm 107:19-20 upon my heart: " 'Lord, help!' they cried in their trouble, and he saved them from their distress. He spoke, and they were healed—snatched from the door of death."

I started reading this Scripture to Mom. I asked her to forgive Dad so she could be healed. God then led me to pray the Scripture in Philippians 4:13—"I can do everything with the help of Christ who gives me the strength I need"—with Mom each day. I asked her to believe it, to say it in her mind. "Mom, I'm going to say this Scripture to you every day, as often as I can, until you can speak it out loud. Start with one word at a time and repeat it in your mind until you can say the entire verse. I know you can do this, Mom!"

We had a morning ritual. I'd call her on the phone, she'd pick it up and listen—but never respond. "Mom, I'm saying this Scripture for you: 'I can do everything...' " After I repeated the verse I'd say, "I'm leaving now, but after I hang up, you think about this verse and just try to say one word. I love you, Mom, and God loves you. Now hang up the phone." She never responded, but I always heard the click.

Though she never communicated that she understood me, I prayed this Scripture for her for the next three years—with no visible sign that it was having any effect. There were many days that I wanted to stop, but as an act of obedience to what the Lord had told me to do, and my strong desire to see Mom get well, I continued.

One day after I had put my sons down for an afternoon nap, I stood at my kitchen sink deep in thought about Mom, when I heard a noise. I turned, and there stood my mother—clean, dressed, and in her right mind.

"Mom!" I cried in shock, "How did you get here?"

"I drove," she said simply. We clung together and cried. My mother was back! But just as God had promised, she wasn't the same.

"I heard everything you said to me but I couldn't answer," Mom said. "I was in a dark place, like a deep well, and couldn't crawl out. I was so afraid you might get discouraged and stop calling and coming over. Quoting those Scriptures to me was my lifeline." Mom's long-imprisoned thoughts began to spill freely.

"I'm sorry that before my illness I called you a fanatic. I didn't understand what a real relationship with Christ was like—I was just a church member. But in my darkness I saw that you really knew God, and I wanted to know Him like you do. I hung onto your every word. Because of your prayers, I accepted Christ and He set me free." We had a lot of catching up to do, and we praised God together as we did.

Mom later told me she had stopped taking all of her medications several weeks prior to that day's miraculous recovery. "I felt like God wanted me to," she explained.

My mother was a transformed woman, free of all bitterness. She resumed her role as wife and homemaker for our disinterested father, but this time without malice. She became active in her women's groups at church, sharing her experiences freely. "For five years I sat imprisoned in my mental hell because of hate. When I finally decided to forgive, God freed me."

The two years following Mom's recovery were the best years of her life. Mom was forgiven of her sins and healed of her mental illness, but physical damage had been done. Though we are free to make choices, we are not free from their consequences. My mom died two years later from cancer at the age of fifty-eight. I believe the years she spent harboring hate predisposed her to this disease process. As a nurse, I have seen many patients with illnesses that show a scientific correlation to stress.

Mom never complained nor indulged in self-pity when she learned she would die from cancer. She embraced her death, for she trusted her Savior completely. Mom left her children and grandchildren a beautiful legacy: "We should forgive those who hurt us or we will be imprisoned by our hate and bitterness." —Winnie Starnes owns and operates Streams in the Desert Adult Care Home in Tempe, Arizona.

But what about those who cause our pain? What is their role in our healing? An important step in overcoming is to realize *we can never control others*. Therefore, we must learn to control our *own* thoughts and actions.

Yes, it would be helpful if those who hurt us would assume responsibility, acknowledge their wrongs, and ask our forgiveness. But it isn't necessary. To say that our healing is dependent upon the willingness of the one who hurt us to engage in group therapy and bare all, or even to just one-on-one admit and accept responsibility for our pain, places us again in the hands of our tormentors. What if they refuse?

My father never admitted his physical and mental abuse to me, but that was his problem—not mine. Dad is accountable to God for his choices, just as I am for mine. Nothing he did nor failed to do can limit my reasoning power. And it was my choice to be an overcomer—not merely a survivor.

Chapter Fourteen

Letting Go

> I read recently there is an identity crisis everywhere. Americans are seeking to find out who they are, where they're coming from, what they're made of—and how they can lose ten to twenty pounds of it.
>
> —James Dent, Charleston, West Virginia *Gazette*

We may not need to lose ten to twenty pounds, but most of us need to lose some heavy negative mental baggage. Letting go may sound like a passive thing to do, but it isn't. It takes courage, strength, and faith.

A climber fell off a cliff. As he tumbled down into the huge canyon, he grabbed hold of a branch of a small tree.

"Help!" he shouted. "Is there anyone up there?"

A deep, majestic voice from the sky echoed through the canyon. "I will help you, my son. But first you must have faith and trust me."

"All right, all right—I trust you," answered the man.

The voice replied, "Let go of the branch."

There was a long pause, and the man shouted again, "Is there anyone else up there?"

Too often we call out to God and when He responds we don't like His answer. We look around for some other source of help. But He is the Great Physician—who better knows our needs? Why do we reject His prescription for pain and refuse to let go? Because we are weak. Only the strong can let go and follow God's leading.

> The strength of a man consists in finding out the way God is going, and going that way.
>
> —Henry Ward Beecher

> It doesn't take a lot of strength to hang on. It takes a lot of strength to let go.
>
> —Rep. J.C. Watts, Jr., in *Time*

We have trouble letting go because we are all tangled up in our baggage. We want to get free but we aren't sure how.

Many of us are trying. We attend Bible studies, read books, and listen to tapes. We are busy learning. But how long does it take to learn the principles that can help us change? Not that long. The only way we can shed the bad habits that keep us earthbound is to exercise the principles we learn.

Let's assume that you weigh thirty pounds too much and you ask God to help you lose weight. You don't exercise, nor do you change your eating habits. But you pray every day begging God to help you lose weight.

How many pounds do you think you would lose? What's the matter, don't you believe in prayer?

God will help us do what we need to do, but He won't do it for us. Many survivors do not become overcomers because it takes hard work, and they are not willing to pay the price. A healthy, happy, proper mental attitude does not simply occur because we wish for it. We can pray for it, yes, but we must do our part before God will do His.

> Therefore, since we are surrounded by such a huge crowd of witnesses to the life of faith, let us strip off every weight that slows us down, especially the sin that so easily hinders our progress. And let us run with endurance the race that God has set before us (Hebrews 12:1).

What is your weight? Not your physical weight, but the negative weight that drags you down.

WORKOUT TIME!

Just prior to my fortieth birthday I joined a gym. The instructor spent considerable time explaining my exercise routine and demonstrating the use of each exercise machine. She also stressed the importance of changing my eating habits.

After observing my workouts for several days, she was confident I understood the routine and concentrated on other newcomers. I never missed a day, I watched my diet, and I worked out diligently. Some time later, I noticed the instructor watching my every move. She walked over and said something I did not want to hear.

"I've been observing your workout—and you're performing that exercise incorrectly."

My heart sank. "I've been sweating through that routine for over a month. You mean I've been wasting my time?" I whined.

"So far as getting the desired results, yes."

She then showed me the correct way, stating that she had shown me how to perform that particular exercise several times when I'd first joined the gym. For some reason I had slipped into my own way of doing it.

"When you do it like this," she said, demonstrating the incorrect way, "you actually exercise the wrong muscles. I'm surprised you didn't notice—that's why we have mirrors in here," she chided gently.

I set to work trying to do the exercise correctly. I soon discovered, however, it was difficult to change because the "muscle memory" went automatically into the wrong exercise motions. It took deliberate concentration to perform the correct movements.

Driving home that day I reflected on a recent discovery. I was turning into a critical person. I hadn't paid much attention—it began so subtly, but I seemed to be getting worse. *Now I understand,* I thought sadly. *I've been exercising my brain incorrectly! I'm becoming good at finding flaws in people.*

It was about that time I had become interested in the power of "self-talk"—what we say to ourselves. I had just acquired a dynamic tape series by a motivational speaker friend who encouraged us to take control of our self-talk. One of the tapes challenged us to a thirty-day mental exercise test. We were to select someone who irritated us—mate, boss, coworker, friend, whomever—and think no critical thoughts about that person for thirty days.

At that particular time in my life, the person who irritated me the most was my husband.

I can't recall what first prompted those critical thoughts—a midlife crisis, dealing with two teenagers, financial pressures, or just the wear and tear of married life—or it could have been my own self-centeredness. Each day I mentally talked to myself about the perceived shortcomings of my husband. With each "discussion," my critical thoughts multiplied and grew stronger. And I disliked him more. I became concerned and took the matter to God.

"Lord, my marriage to Jerry is a lifetime commitment, and right now I feel like that's a death sentence. I don't want a divorce, but I can't stand the thought of living in a loveless marriage for the rest of my life. Would you please help me change my attitude toward him? You helped me to forgive my father, so will you help me love Jerry as I once did?"

Now remember the example where we asked God to help us lose thirty pounds? You know, where we discussed how we must do our part by managing our diet and exercising? Well, we now understand that God would not answer my prayer until I did my part. That tape series entered my life at the perfect time, for it outlined my needed mental exercise routine.

The challenge was to kick out all negative thoughts about Jerry (or whomever) for thirty days. Since "all nature abhors a vacuum," I was to fill the space my negative thoughts had occupied with positive thoughts. I was not to replace one unkind thought with one kind thought—I was to replace one unkind thought with ten kind thoughts! Ten good qualities that described my husband.

This is called "the principle of dilution." If you take a glass half filled with cola and pour water into it until it overflows and you keep pouring, eventually the cola will be gone and you will have a glass of pure, clean water.

I had recently attended a seminar where this concept was vividly demonstrated. The instructor spoke about how we should concentrate upon something we want and not upon what we don't want. To illustrate his point, the instructor stopped and said, "Despite what I say during the next few minutes, I want you to use all of your powers of concentration to not listen to the ceiling fan."

Until that moment I'd not been aware of the noisy ceiling fan. How was it possible that I had not heard it before? His point was well made, for the more I concentrated on not listening to the fan, the more aware I became of it—and the louder the sound.

Gradually, I became so interested in the new information the instructor presented that I literally sat on the edge of my chair waiting for his next word. I was so absorbed in what I wanted to hear that my mind blocked out what I didn't want to hear. The noisy fan was forgotten until he again reminded us of its sound and his point was further proved.

God created our brain as a goal-striving mechanism to help us achieve whatever goal we focus upon. That is why our thoughts are so important. We can study medicine and become a lifesaving surgeon or we can study weapons of destruction and become a terrorist. The mechanics of the mind function impartially.

But back to my challenge. I soon discovered it would take longer than thirty days. The rule was that whenever you failed you had to start all over again—from day one. I worked and worked and went two weeks without letting one negative thought get a foothold in my mind. I was ecstatic. The very next day, I suffered a major setback and I had to start all over again.

"Oh, no! Lord, at this rate it's going to be a lifelong task for me."

"Bingo!" said the Holy Spirit.

I finally made my goal. Thirty wonderful days without one energy-leaking negative thought about my husband! What amazed me more than that accomplishment, however, was how much Jerry had improved during that short period of time! More importantly, I had developed a lifelong practice that became the norm for me rather than the exception.

Of course we are not to use this practice as a form of self-denial—a way to avoid conflict when our mate or someone else has flagrantly violated or abused us in some way and needs to be held accountable. I'm talking about freeing ourselves of the plain old nitpicking critical habit of looking for flaws in others.

FRUITS OF THE SPIRIT DON'T INCLUDE CRABAPPLES

> But when the Holy Spirit controls our lives, he will produce this kind of fruit in us: love, joy, peace, patience, kindness, goodness, faithfulness, gentleness, and self-control.
>
> —Galatians 5:22

Who in their right mind wouldn't want to be loving, joyful, at peace with God and man, patient, kind, good, faithful, gentle, and self-controlled? Why don't more of us produce good fruits? Because we are not in the right mind.

How can we be loving while thinking hateful thoughts?

How can we be joyful while dwelling in self-pity?

How can we know peace while harboring resentment?

How can we be patient while demanding our way immediately?

How can we be kind while planning revenge?

How can we be good while entertaining bad thoughts?

How can we be faithful while living in disobedience?

How can we be gentle while harboring combative thoughts?

And how can we produce fruit of the Spirit without using self-control?

The only way we can reap a bountiful harvest is to control our thoughts and feelings, but we can't do it without help.

> So I advise you to live according to your new life in the Holy Spirit. Then you won't be doing what you sinful nature craves. The old sinful nature loves to do evil, which is just opposite form what the Holy Spirit wants. And the Spirit gives us desires that are opposite from what the sinful nature desires. These two forces are constantly fighting each other, and your choices are never free from this conflict (Galatians 5:16-17).

Living in the Spirit is not a passive existence where we just fold our hands and pray, waiting for the fruit of the Spirit to drop in our laps like overripe fruit, honors bestowed upon the worthy—like the gold stars we won for perfect attendance in Sunday school. Awards for just showing up.

The fruit of the Spirit are character traits, formed in the fiery furnace of daily experience. They come to us not as rewards but as results, developed through hand-to-hand combat upon the battlefield of our mind. Ours is no minor conflict, for we fight in a life-and-death struggle against powerful evil forces that seek to control our mind.

> For we are not fighting against people made of flesh and blood, but against the evil rulers and authorities of the unseen world, against those mighty powers of darkness who rule this world, and against wicked spirits in the heavenly realms (Ephesians 6:12).

God tells us not only to struggle with our thoughts but also to take them as captives.

> We destroy every proud obstacle that keeps people from knowing God. We capture their rebellious thoughts and teach them to obey Christ (2 Corinthians 10:5).

So think clearly and exercise self-control (1 Peter 1:13).

TRUTH OR CONSEQUENCES

We do not have to accept every thought that pops into our mind, nor do we have to verbalize it. Jesus recognized the subtle method of temptation through thoughts voiced by others. Let's consider what happened during a conversation between Jesus and Peter in the eighth chapter of Mark.

> Then Jesus began to tell them that he, the Son of Man, would suffer many terrible things and be rejected by the leaders, the leading priests, and the teachers of religious law. He would be killed, and three days later he would rise again. As he talked about this openly with his disciples, Peter took him aside and told him he shouldn't say things like that (Mark 8:31-32).

Peter loved Jesus deeply. He experienced a sudden memory loss, however, regarding God's prophecy requirements when he tried to detour Jesus from the road to Calvary. The Scriptures do not tell us what Peter said, but I can only imagine what I might have said had I been Peter.

> Surely You can't mean this, Lord? You are the Messiah! What earthly good will it

> do for You to give up the cause now, at the peak of Your career, and let evil men kill You? What kind of testimony is that to the world? I'll tell You—they'll think You're weak, that You're not who You say you are. Your chosen people are counting on You, and You're going to let them down? Get a grip, Jesus. This martyr stuff sounds good, but what will it accomplish in the long run? Can't You do what is right without doing Yourself in?

And what was Jesus' response to Peter's rebuke? "Jesus turned and looked at his disciples and then said to Peter very sternly, 'Get away from me, Satan! You are seeing things merely from a human point of view, not from God's' " (Mark 8:33).

I don't know how else to interpret this Scripture other than to believe that Satan used Peter's mind to house his evil thoughts. And Peter, being an indiscriminating messenger at that moment, delivered it straight to the Messiah, without even questioning the message.

Jesus loved Peter, but He instantly recognized Satan's sneaky tactic in Peter's rebuke. Jesus knew that Satan's goal was to keep Him from the cross, and what better way than to use one of Jesus' own disciples?

Peter meant well, but is it possible that part of his passion to protect Jesus from the cross stemmed from his own personal ambitions? At that time in his ministry, Peter may have felt that he had not left his all to follow someone who claimed to be the Messiah, only to have his hopes dashed on a cross.

Since Peter did not test the thoughts that popped into his mind against the Scripture, they escaped through his mouth in the form of a rebuke. Many of us have that problem. We would like to follow the saying, "Be sure brain is engaged before putting mouth into motion," but most often we are more apt to "open mouth, insert foot." We need to exercise caution when advising others as to what they should or shouldn't do by carefully assessing our thoughts on the subject before opening our mouth.

Likewise, we need to develop our ability to recognize satanic suggestions as quickly as did Jesus, regardless of how logical or well-meaning they sound. We have no way of knowing, of course, the motive behind what others say, but we can test our thoughts and motives.

How do we test them? Against God's Word and the Holy Spirit at work within us. The problem for many of us is that we are not well equipped with the Word. We rarely read it, much less study it enough to test our thoughts against it. "I have hidden your word in my heart, that I might not sin against you" (Psalm 119:11).

Memorization of the words are helpful, but even more powerful is the absorption of their truth into our mind. We can then live by the principles of God's truth even when specific verses can't be recalled. We can then test our thoughts against God's principles. If a thought leads us away from God, it is a lie and should be banished.

We can't let one evil thought into our mental camp to warm its hands by the fire of our imagination. It will catch us off guard and destroy us. A single thought can produce feelings, and feelings can result in actions. What harm can one evil thought produce?

I listened to a tape in which the speaker talked of a man who was interviewed in his prison cell. When asked why he had committed his crime, he related this story: "I worked at a construction site where every day children passed by on their way to school. One day I saw this little girl. At first," he said, "I just noticed how cute she was. Every day I watched her go by. Then one day, a strange thought popped into my mind: 'I wonder what it would feel like to caress her.'" The man said the next day when he saw her, the thought popped into his mind again. And again the next day, and the next. Until late one afternoon, when he had the opportunity, he raped and then killed the little girl.

What a tragic action resulting from a single thought— entertained and not rejected.

> Every thought seed sown or allowed to fall into the mind, and to take root there, produces its own, blossoming sooner or later into act, and bearing its own fruitage of opportunity and circumstance. Good thoughts bear good fruit, bad thoughts bad fruit.
>
> —James Allen, *As a Man Thinketh*

BUT I CAN'T HELP THE WAY I FEEL!

Just as we are to test our thoughts, we are to test our feelings. For surviving victims, negative feelings often occur from a trigger reflex. Sometimes, without conscious thought, a situation reminds us of a painful past experience and our feelings are triggered, and we aren't even sure why.

Even into adulthood, I cried when I heard a puppy whimper or yelp. This was triggered automatically by my painful childhood memory experienced when I discovered the bodies of our tiny puppies, killed by our father during the night.

For years I cried when a court scene appeared on TV or in a movie, triggered by my painful memories of Dad's trial. These were triggered responses, occurring instantly without forethought. Even though they had occurred spontaneously, conscious thoughts of resentment toward my father flooded my mind—the father whom I had forgiven.

The most difficult problem we face in forgetting past pain is learning to deal with an emotional system that has been programmed a certain way for so long that our feelings can't respond appropriately on demand.

Following a luncheon one day, a woman asked, "How often do you have to forgive your father?"

"What do you mean? I forgave him only once."

"I forgave my mother for her drunken abuse years ago," she explained, "but sometimes when I think of her I get angry—and I have to forgive her again. Some of my friends say I haven't really forgiven her if I get mad when I think of her. And please don't suggest counseling—I've gone to counselors for years. What I need to know is why do I continue to get angry at her when I think I've forgiven her?"

"Were you sincere when you forgave her?"

"Yes."

"Are you sure?"

"Definitely!"

"Forgiveness is a choice and has nothing to do with feelings. Either we forgive or we don't. You say that you were sincere, so forgiveness for your mother is a fact. Feelings, however, are not always based on fact. They are real, yes, but they may have little to do with our present reality. Your feelings of anger were appropriate at one time, but once you forgave your mother they became inappropriate. You need to reject them each time you feel them."

"But I can't control my feelings."

"Are you sure about that?" I asked. "Were you ever deeply in love with another man before you married your husband?"

"Yes."

"Did you ever run into him accidentally after you were married?"

"Yes."

"How did you feel? Be honest."

Her face flushed. "I was surprised at how quickly those old romantic feelings resurfaced. I love my husband very much and am happily married, but I was shocked at how I felt. My hands actually became sweaty with excitement. I remember thinking, 'I'm so glad I had my hair done today.'" Embarrassed at her admission, she lowered her eyes. "I actually hoped that he still found me attractive."

"Those were natural feelings," I said. "What I want to know is, what did you do with them?"

"What do you mean?"

"Those warm, romantic, fuzzy feelings feel good. Didn't you revel in them, relive those past memories, go over and over them in your mind for months afterward?"

"Of course not—I got rid of them as fast as I could!" she exclaimed.

"Why would you want to do that? They were just harmless feelings."

"Because it's not right. I'm married and those feelings are wrong now. Besides, I wouldn't want my husband drooling over some old flame. There could be problems."

"So what you're saying," I said, "is that you controlled your feelings by rejecting them."

She smiled. "Yes, I guess that's what I did."

"We can do the same thing with our past negative feelings. Just as the romantic feelings can cause problems if they are entertained, so too can old feelings of anger and resentment. It may be more difficult, however, to reject them because we've probably entertained them for years. We relive those negative feelings over and over, not because we enjoy them, but because we don't know how to get rid of them. Once we learn how, we are freed from their power."

"How did you do it?"

"I made a conscious decision to deal with them. Each time they popped up, I said to myself, almost angrily, 'I don't like these feelings, and I won't tolerate them!' Try it, you'll be amazed! I do that with any feelings I don't like—fear, anxiety, whatever. Another way I dealt with them was to place a circle in my mind, write *anger* in the center, and draw a slash through it—like a 'don't smoke' sign. It doesn't matter the method, just decide what works best for you, then do it consistently, until the feelings never return."

ANYONE CAN DO IT

Shortly after we were married, Jerry and I hiked up to the Old Fremont Trail above Santa Barbara, California, with my mom and a friend. We briefly relived history as we recalled how General Fremont led his wagon trains across that range of mountains. We stared, amazed at the foot deep trail cut in solid stone, made by countless wagon wheels, each following the other in the same rut. It was easier for the wagon drivers to ride in the ruts than to try to get out. Fortunately, the ruts led in the right direction.

It takes even greater effort to get out of a mental rut. Our choice of thoughts provides the vehicle that will keep us in the rut or empower us to climb out.

I was discussing the importance of monitoring our thoughts and feelings one day with a Christian friend who was a survivor but not yet an overcomer. She responded crisply, "Well, that sounds an awful lot like mind control to me."

"That's exactly what it is!" I said excitedly. Her eyes narrowed as I continued. "Would you start your car engine, drive it onto the freeway at full speed, and then let go of the steering wheel?"

"Of course not!"

"Why not?"

"That's obvious," she said. "The car would go out of control."

"That's my point. Most of my life I lived out of control. I allowed circumstances and negative feelings to steer my mind. They prevented me from getting to where I wanted to go by driving me into places I didn't want to be. Then I sat there like a helpless victim, blaming everyone else for the spot I was in and complaining, 'Why me?' Finally, I am beginning to take control of something precious that God gave me for my use alone—my mind. If I don't control it, someone else or circumstances will."

Many people feel that the overcomers they know or hear about are unique, a cut above other victims who were destined to live in the pit. They are convinced that these overcomers are favored by God with a special gift or ability to overcome tragedies. They suspect that the overcomer never suffered as much as they did or they wouldn't be able to climb out. But that is not true. God never shows partiality when it comes to giving His grace, strength, and power.

Many of us have walked in our rut for so long it has become our comfort zone—our Fremont Trail rut. We feel safe there between its strong sides. Sure, we are miserable, but at least we know what to expect—even if it is only more of the same. The familiar may feel safe, but it can destroy us. At some point our particular rut may run us off the edge of the mountain. When that happens, for fear that we will crash below, we too often grasp just any branch we think can help us.

We may cling to a habit that seems to temporarily ease our pain and numb our heartaches, but in the end it will destroy our health and relationships and detour us from reaching our potential. And it could destroy us. "There is a path before each person that seems right, but it ends in death" (Proverbs 16:25).

The good news is, no habit or lifestyle is impossible to break once we make the decision to let it go—and seek God's direction.

But what if we see the need to let go but we are frightened? We suspect that if we are to become an overcomer we must change our way of thinking, and that is scary. We have programmed ourselves to react, not act. The thought of traveling a new road that demands taking responsibility for our thoughts and actions terrifies us. The overcomer's road looks much rougher and harder than does the victim's passive path. And we are not sure we want to pay the price.

Besides, we don't even know where to begin.

So now the LORD says, Stop right where you are! look for the old, godly way, and walk in it. Travel its path, and you will find rest for your souls (Jeremiah 6:16).

CHAPTER FIFTEEN

A Three-Step Process

> There are only two ways to approach life—as a victim or as a gallant fighter—and you must decide if you want to act or react... a lot of people forget that.
>
> —Merle Shain

> Don't let evil conquer you, but conquer evil by doing good (Romans 12:21).

> To everyone who is victorious I will give fruit from the tree of life in the paradise of God (Revelation 2:7).

What is the difference between surviving and overcoming?

Survive: to continue to exist or live after.

Overcome: to get the better of, overpower, overwhelm, to gain superiority.

Can we survive tragic circumstances, discard the negative effects of our experiences, and go on to became gallant warriors? Can we overpower our hate and resentment and overwhelm the tragedies of life with love, forgiveness, and a superior healthy outlook? Yes.

THE SURVIVOR

Many people survive unbelievably difficult circumstances, and we are amazed at their strong will and tenacity. I'm sure you can think of several people like this. Surviving is a wonderful thing, but we can't stop there. Sadly, many survivors never become overcomers. They exist, but they don't live—not in the full sense of the word.

Hiding our pain inside where it can eat away the precious core of life is not living. Venting our resentment and anger upon others also is not living.

Neither is it living when we rely on the continual sympathy of those around us. If we depend upon the short-term rush we get from pity from others as a permanent cure, we are headed for trouble. Some survivors become addicted to the "warm fuzzies" of sympathy.

My mother, once a vibrant and happy woman, became addicted to pity. Year after year, she gave daily "pity parties" where she displayed her emotional wounds. The problem was, in order to hold the attention of friends who had heard her story many times (and to keep them from running away), she had to embellish her story with new shock material, often fabricated. Such is the danger of a victim hooked on pity.

A certain amount of sympathy is helpful, but at its best, pity should be nothing more than a temporary balm to soothe our pain. At its worst, it is a dangerous substitute for personal accountability. We are not entitled to a lifetime contract of sympathy because of past pains. Thinking otherwise traps us in a victim mentality.

My mother was a remarkable survivor, but sadly she never became an overcomer. One would think that Mom would have been bitter and hateful while imprisoned for twenty-one years in an abusive marriage. To the contrary, she was laughter, light, and love for us in our bleak circumstances.

Following Dad's imprisonment and our flight to California, we children wanted to enjoy our newfound freedom, but Mother wanted to focus upon her past pain.

Mom was wise about caring for her health. No recreational drugs, no cigarettes, no alcohol, and very little caffeine. If only she had exercised caution about what she fed her mind! Plastic surgery restored Mother's beauty and she began dating, but inwardly she was turning into something ugly.

Mom had trusted Christ with her heart and life three months before Dad's final attempt upon her life, but now she seldom attended church. That was understandable since she was angry at God. She felt He had abandoned her.

"Where was God when I needed Him the most?" she snarled one day, eyes snapping.

"God was there with you," I replied. "How do you think you survived?" I asked, my patience wearing thin.

"Because I refused to die—I wouldn't give him that satisfaction! My hate helped me survive," she hissed.

"Yes, Mom, hate can motivate a person to live, but hate can also destroy you. God loved you then and He loves you now. He's waiting for you to let Him fill you with His peace—as we kids have experienced."

"Peace? God wants me to have peace? Then why doesn't He strike Clyde Crawley with a bolt of lightning? I'll have peace when he drops dead."

But Mother was wrong. Years later, following Dad's death, peace never came. She simply transferred her hate to others.

Ten years before her death, I thought Mom was ready to leave her desert of discontent. She told me that after listening to a Christian radio program, she realized that God had not deserted her when she was almost murdered by Dad.

"I finally understand that God didn't abandon me. He kept me alive that night, just like the doctors said. They called it a miracle. And all this time I've been blaming God."

"I know, Mom," I said. "It's easy to blame God. We blame Him when others hurt us and we blame Him when we hurt ourselves. But through it all, He loves us anyway."

I hugged her and added, "Some day I pray you'll give your hurts to God. He can help again, if you let Him."

She suddenly stiffened. "If by that you mean I should forgive Clyde Crawley, forget it. I'll never forgive him!"

And she didn't. But her choice destroyed her health and broke our hearts.

Despite the devotion of our stepfather Ira, a caring husband for over thirty-five years, Mother found nothing for which to be thankful. She made his life miserable as she spewed forth hate for our father and anyone who didn't agree with her.

Hoping that a godly psychologist might help, we children suggested counseling. We were surprised and excited when she agreed. Our excitement was short-lived when we realized her only reason for going was to gain support in her battle to convince us that we were wrong in forgiving our father and she was right in not forgiving him.

When the psychologist didn't say what she wanted to hear, she stopped going.

Could Mom have been different? I believe the answer is yes. She was stable in every area except on the subject of our father and the past. She held positions with companies in California that required intelligence far beyond her fourth grade education. On her job applications she claimed a high school education, but her performance level was equivalent to that of a college graduate.

Could God have helped our mother overcome her past? Scripture says He can. "Give all your worries and cares to God, for he cares about you" (1 Peter 5:7). "But forget all that—it is nothing compared to what I am going to do. For I am about to do something new. See, I have already begun!" (Isaiah 43:18-19).

We can choose to humble ourselves, seek and accept Christ's help, or we can reject His offer. But if we refuse, we will be the losers. "But if you rebel against the LORD's commands and refuse to listen to him, then his hand will be as heavy upon you..." (1 Samuel 12:15). "Yet they kept on sinning against him, rebelling against the Most High in the desert" (Psalm 78:17).

The children of Israel were only fourteen miles from their promised land of rest, but because of their grumbling lack of faith, they wandered in the desert for forty years. They did not believe God could protect them from the "giants" in the land that He had promised to give them. When they finally repented and sought God, He led them into their land of abundance and rest.

Because Mom focused on her giants of hate and resentment, she, too, wandered in her desert for over forty years before she was taken into her promised land upon her death. Finally, she had peace—in the arms of her Savior who understood. The forgiveness He had given her so long ago was not rescindable. I'm sure they wept tears of joy as He embraced her in welcome. But I wonder—could some of their tears have been for her wasted years in the desert? "I am the LORD your God, who teaches you what is good for you and leads you along the paths you should follow. Oh, that you had listened to my commands! Then you would have had peace flowing like a gentle river and righteousness rolling over you like waves in the sea" (Isaiah 48:17-18).

THE OVERCOMER

Why are there so few overcomers? Because few of us realize the power of the thoughts that fuel our minds. And even fewer realize that we have a choice as to the type of fuel we use.

> Good thoughts and actions can never produce bad results; bad thoughts and actions can never produce good results. This is but saying that nothing can come from corn but corn, nothing from nettles but nettles. Men understand this law in the natural world, and work with it; but few understand it in the mental and moral world (though its operation there is just as simple and undeviating), and they, therefore, do not cooperate with it.
>
> —James Allen, *As a Man Thinketh*

Simply put, if we are obsessed with thoughts of bitterness and hate, we will become bitter and hateful. If we are obsessed with thoughts of kindness and love, we will become kind and loving. We become like our obsessions because our thoughts become our attitudes.

> Men imagine that thought can be kept secret, but it cannot...hateful and condemnatory thoughts crystallize into habits of accusations and violence, which solidify into circumstances of injury and persecution...On the other hand, beautiful thoughts of all kinds crystallize into

> habits of grace and kindliness, which solidify into genial and sunny circumstances...gentle and forgiving thoughts crystallize into habits of gentleness...loving and unselfish thoughts crystallize into habits of self-forgetfulness for others.
>
> —James Allen, *As a Man Thinketh*

Mr. Allen has fleshed out for us the truth of the old Scripture which tells is that whatever we think, that is what we are.

Another wise man wrote the following:

ATTITUDES

> Words can never adequately convey the incredible impact of our attitude toward life. The longer I live the more convinced I become that life is 10 percent what happens to us and 90 percent how we respond to it.
>
> I believe the single most significant decision I can make on a day-to-day basis is my choice of attitude. It is more important than my past, my education, my bankroll, my successes or failures, fame or pain, what other people think of me or say about me, my circumstances, or my position. Attitude keeps me going

> or cripples my progress. It alone fuels my fire or assaults my hope. When my attitudes are right, there's no barrier too high, no valley too deep, no dream too extreme, no challenge too great for me.
>
> —*Strengthening Your Grip*, by Charles R. Swindoll ©1982 W Publishing Group (formerly Word, Inc.), Nashville, TN. Used by permission.

Viktor Frankl, a distinguished psychiatrist and survivor of unspeakable atrocities in Auschwitz, a World War II Nazi concentration camp, had this to say about attitude:

> The last of the human freedoms is to choose one's attitude in any given set of circumstances...Man is ultimately self-determining. What he becomes—within the limits of endowment and environment—he has made out of himself. In the concentration camps, for example, in this living laboratory and on this testing ground, we watched and witnessed some of our comrades behave like swine while others behaved like saints. Man has both potentialities within himself: which one is actualized depends on decisions but not on conditions.
>
> —*Man's Search For Meaning*

While few of us will experience atrocities such as were experienced by Dr. Frankl, each of us experiences heartache. It matters not the cause of our pain; all pain hurts, and we feel helpless. What can we do when we feel paralyzed by our circumstances? How can we move past being survivors to become overcomers? I hope the next few chapters will help to start you on the path to overcoming past hurts, great or small, that are preventing you from truly living.

STORY OF AN OVERCOMER

My friend Linda Turkiewicz is an overcomer. She relates the following story of what she did when she was utterly helpless.

> Frederic, my husband of four years, jammed his gun to my head and sneered, "Now we'll see how tough this stubborn German-Irish gal really is!" He pulled the trigger. I heard the empty chamber click. "Don't you like Russian roulette?" he asked, laughing. "Let's try it again." Twice I had heard an empty click. I closed my eyes and flinched as he cocked the trigger for the third time, waiting for the inevitable bullet to penetrate my skull and

end it all. My life began to flash before my mind's eyes.

I had survived childhood polio and, despite doctors' predictions that I would be wheelchair-bound, had learned to walk again using braces and crutches. I met Frederic at college, and we fell in love and married. Though doctors said I couldn't have children, we had two beautiful miracle girls, Michelle and Monique. Life had been wonderful —what happened?

As a lab supervisor at a busy hospital, Frederic worked long hours. He began staying away from home even more, volunteering to work extra shifts. He took drugs to stay awake, then other drugs to help him sleep. He began to change. At first the changes were subtle, then they progressed until he became a stranger—a stranger who was now trying to kill me.

The gun clicked a third time. Again, an empty chamber. I opened my eyes as he suddenly lowered the gun. Without a word, he turned, walked into his bedroom, and shut the door.

The next morning Frederic was gone. We didn't know it then, but we would not hear from him for seventeen years. I did know, however, that it was up to me to get a job and raise my girls. I found work at a local hospital and eventually became administrator to several medical clinics in Scottsdale, Arizona. Finally, life was good again.

Then one day while I was riding with a friend, a drunken driver ran a red light and broadsided our car on the passenger side. I had severe head wounds and facial lacerations that would require plastic surgery. Worse yet, I suffered severe injuries to my sternum area and to both arms. I could no longer use crutches, and because my legs were useless, I was confined to a wheelchair—just as the doctors had predicted when I was eight years old.

I couldn't drive and had to be transported everywhere. I was dependent upon others. Suddenly, this tough German-Irish gal was helpless and without hope. I knew I couldn't overcome this by myself. And was I angry! *Why me, God? Haven't I always taken care of myself? And haven't I been a good moral person?* But God didn't answer.

One day my demands gave way to pleas for help. *Please, God, help me. I can't make it alone.* This time, God an-

> swered. He flooded my life with loving Christians. They took me to church, to Christian Women's Club luncheons, and finally to a women's retreat where I yielded my life to Christ as my Savior and Lord. I was no longer alone. I even forgave Frederic and was freed from resentment.

For over thirty-three years Linda has directed children's ministries and currently is working with children in Greeley, Co. Her husband, Mark, has helped her experience jet skiing, wheelchair tennis, basketball, and camping. Her daughters and their husbands have presented them with two granddaughters.

Linda is a dynamic overcomer—she says not just because she is a tough German-Irish gal survivor, but because she trusted God.

THE OVERCOMER'S JOURNEY: A THREE-STEP PROCESS

We have learned the difference between survivors and overcomers. We have read true stories of overcomers. We will now take a closer, in-depth look at the attitude of an overcomer.

The personal experiences and growth patterns of all overcomers are varied, but I believe the three steps listed below will enable anyone to overcome anything—even the most tragic circumstances in life—and emerge as a living marvel. There can be no lovelier gift to give back to our heavenly Father.

> My life is an example to many, because you have been my strength and protection. That is why I can never stop praising you; I declare your glory all day long (Psalms 71:7-8).

Below, in a nutshell, is the three-step process from survivor to overcomer.

Step One: Forgiveness—Forgiveness has three parts:

(1) We must accept forgiveness from God,
(2) We must offer forgiveness to others, and
(3) We must forgive ourselves.

Step Two: Accountability—We must assume responsibility for our thoughts and actions.

Step Three: Gratitude—We must cultivate an "attitude of gratitude."

The next three chapters will take you through the three steps in an in-depth way. Your life doesn't have to be a ruin because of the difficult things in your past! Read on, and find the positive, fulfilling future God has for you.

CHAPTER SIXTEEN

Step One: Forgiveness

I believe the first and most important step toward a happy and fulfilling life is forgiveness—a threefold process. The first part of Step One, receiving God's forgiveness, is imperative for it involves not only our present life but also our eternal life. But if we skip parts two and three of Step One, we will remain mere survivors.

A. God's gift of forgiveness to us. The single most important act of my life was addressing my personal need for forgiveness by God. This was accomplished through my acceptance of Christ. (Remember? He is the only antidote for our inherited tainted blood line and our personal sins.) "Because one person disobeyed God, many became sinners. But because one other person obeyed God, many will be made righteous" (Romans 5:19). "But if we confess our sins to him, he is faithful and just to forgive us our sins and to cleanse us from all wickedness" (1 John 1:9).

I mentioned in chapter two how I took this first step and humbly asked God to forgive my sins. We Christians speak of "giving our heart" to Jesus, but we also give Him at that moment our sins, our broken dreams, and our pains. We can't carry these burdens any longer, so we trust Him to lift them and deal with them. He then creates in us a new heart. "Create in me a clean heart, O God. Renew a loyal spirit within me" (Psalm 51:10).

If you are seriously interested in accepting Christ into your life, let me tell you how easy it is. Just pray from your heart the words that are presented in the prayer below, or use your own words. Sounds too easy, you say? The truth is, God *does* make it easy for us because He's already done the *hard* part. It's our mistaken ideas that make it seem difficult. But whether my words or yours, make them sincere—straight from *your* heart.

Dear God,

I'm not sure I understand everything I've heard or read about You, but one thing I do understand is that I am a sinner and that Christ died for my sins so I wouldn't have to. I confess my sins to You and ask You to forgive me. Please create in me a new heart, for I want You in my life forever.

In Jesus' name I pray.

Amen

God not only creates in us a new heart, He does much more. He gives us new life and power by sending the Holy Spirit to dwell within us. Never again can anything overcome us. His Spirit helps, guides, and comforts us. When no one understands how we feel, not even our mate or closest friends, the Holy Spirit does—because He knows our heart. He even helps us pray when we can't find the right words.

> And the Holy Spirit helps us in our weakness. For example, we don't know what God wants us to pray for. But the Holy Spirit prays for us with groanings that cannot be expressed in words. And the Father who knows all hearts knows what the Spirit is saying, for the Spirit pleads for us believers in harmony with God's own will (Romans 8:26-27).

B. We must forgive others. So far, God has done all the giving. He rescued me from my tainted bloodline through the fresh and pure blood transfusion supplied by Christ, He forgave my sins, He instilled the Holy Spirit within me to comfort and to guide me, and He is preparing an eternal dwelling place for me.

> There is more than enough room in my Father's home. If this were not so, would

> I have told you that I am going to prepare a place for you? When everything is ready, I will come and get you, so that you will always be with me where I am (John 14:2-3).

What have I given God thus far, other than my sins and my broken heart to be made new? Nothing. What can I give Him? A life that honors Him. I must be willing to do for others what He has done for me. How can those who sin against me believe that God, whom they have not met, will forgive them their sins if I, whom they *have* met, won't? My forgiveness helps provide evidence that God will do what He says He will do.

It is easier to accept forgiveness than it is to give it. We make the act of forgiving difficult because we focus on the disobedience of the one who hurt us rather than our need to be obedient to the One who forgave us. Maybe we need a clearer understanding of why we are to forgive. We are to forgive out of love and gratitude to God because He forgave us, because He expects it, because Christ set the example, and because the Holy Spirit enables us.

Jesus said,

> Father, forgive them, for they don't know what they are doing (Luke 23:34).

> But when you are praying, first forgive anyone you are holding a grudge against, so that your Father in heaven will forgive your sins, too (Mark 11:25).

> We are most like beasts when we kill. We are most like men when we judge. We are most like God when we forgive.
>
> —Author unknown

> To err is human, to forgive divine.
>
> —Alexander Pope

> The weak can never forgive. Forgiveness is the attribute of the strong.
>
> —Mahatma Gandhi

> Forgiveness is not an emotion...Forgiveness is an act of the will, and the will can function regardless of the temperature of the heart.
>
> —Corrie ten Boom

C. We must forgive ourselves. Maybe you have no trouble forgiving others but you can't forgive yourself. Somehow you feel to blame for all the pain you've experienced, or you feel shame that you couldn't do more to change the circumstances. You wonder if you invited the tragedies that occurred. You let the perpetrator place his guilt upon you and you still carry the heavy shame upon your back. Maybe you *have* committed some terrible sins. (Who among us hasn't!)They hang around your neck like an albatross and you berate yourself daily. The origin of your feelings of guilt and shame isn't important. The point is, you don't have to continue carrying them. Ask God to forgive you and He will. And when He does, it's a done deal. You have no right to insult His forgiveness and love by continuing to hate yourself. "I—yes, I alone—will blot out your sins for my own sake and will never think of them again" (Isaiah 43:25).

There is a temptation each of us face when the old feelings of guilt pop up. We start to feel guilty again. Remember how we discussed the ways we can reject old feelings that are no longer valid? We need to do the same thing with those old guilt feelings which are no longer valid. When an old illegitimate guilt feeling grabs us, we should say, "I don't like the way this makes me feel, and I reject it because God has already forgiven me for it—and forgotten it. I am SO thankful that God did that for me!"

CHAPTER SEVENTEEN

Step Two: Accountability

We must assume responsibility for our thoughts and actions. How can we obey God if we don't take control of our thoughts? This is the most difficult of all battles! It is an ongoing, lifetime commitment that requires studying (not just reading) the Bible and praying for understanding—and then putting God's principles into practice.

When I first began to understand the importance of assuming responsibility for my thoughts and actions, I was struck by a quote I read which described me perfectly:

> Men are disturbed, not by the things that happen, but by their opinion of the things that happen.
>
> —Epictetus, ancient philosopher

So impressed was I with this statement that I typed copies of it and taped them to the mirrors in my bathrooms as reminders for me to not react to everything but to seek the truth in every situation. The following is an example.

As I walked down our local street one day, a member of my church walked toward me. I smiled and slowed my pace, ready for a brief chat. But she didn't even break stride, didn't return my smile, and passed me without a word. Those are the bare facts of that brief incident. But just watch what my insecure mind did with that little tidbit of circumstance!

Of all the nerve—she snubbed me! Why? I've done nothing to her. My mind worked overtime trying to uncover the reason I was snubbed. *It must be because I disagreed with her at the committee meeting last week. Well, give me a break! My opinion is just as good as hers—even though I'm not an attorney's wife!* I fumed and worried about it for the rest of the week.

The following Sunday I sat several pews behind her at church. *How can she sit there looking pious after treating me so rudely? What a hypocrite! And I always thought she was such a great Christian! Just goes to show how you never really know about someone.*

Following the service I was engaged in conversation with a friend when I felt a touch on my shoulder. It was the attorney's wife. "I want to apologize for not acknowledging you the other day. I was so deep in thought that I didn't even realize it was you until you had passed by. I'm sorry. I hope you didn't think I deliberately ignored you, for I would never do that."

"Oh—thank you," I stammered in surprise. "No, I didn't give it a second thought," I lied.

I recalled the quote on my mirror. What a perfect example of blowing something out of proportion with my opinion. I was wrong on every count! That incident motivated me to control my thoughts and become more objective and less subjective.

But how could I do that when I wasn't even sure what those words meant? I thought that being objective meant I was against something. Mr. Webster taught me the difference.

Objective: Expressing or involving the use of facts without distortion by personal feelings, prejudices, or interpretations.

Subjective: Knowledge as conditioned by personal mental characteristics or states; modified or affected by personal views, experience, or background.

Example of objective view: Every person is born a unique individual with value and potential, despite race or environment, and that includes me. (This is fact, based not only upon the Bible, but the consensus of rational mankind.)

Example of subjective view: Because I was born into a bad environment, I don't have a chance. I am inferior and don't deserve anything better than my beginning environment. (This view is based upon feelings and totally lacking in fact.)

There are three elements to objectivity: *the acceptance of truth*, *the pursuit of truth*, and *the adjustment to truth.*

Example of the acceptance of truth: I was created by God as a unique person of immense value. I accept the truth that among the billions of individuals already born, and who will be born, there is only one me. God loves me, and I have something to contribute to this world.

Example of the pursuit of truth: No matter how uncomfortable I may be with the truth, I will strive to seek it and to live by it. I will attempt to be honest with myself at all times, for only then can I be honest with others.

Example of the adjustment to truth: I will adjust to the truth by assuming responsibility for my thoughts and actions. I will break the habit of making excuses and blaming others or circumstances for my failures and mistakes. I will do my best to rectify my wrongs and apologize for the mistakes I make—regardless of the cost. I will not curse myself for my errors, but I will learn from them and become stronger.

We must become lovers and seekers of truth. Seeing the truth, however, can be painful, for it always calls for action. That is why we often try to avoid it.

We try to escape from truth by hiding from it.

We eat ourselves into obesity, but are still hungry.

We drink and drug ourselves into emotional and mental derelicts, and remain thirsty.

We try to outrun truth by busying ourselves. We go from one person, party, or activity to another until we are exhausted. We fear that in the vulnerability of being alone, honesty will seduce us and we will be faced with the reality of what we don't want to see.

We plunge into our career, our work, our hobbies, and become overachievers. We seek to build with our hands an image worth viewing, but we never succeed.

We work feverishly behind the walls of religion, observing mindless rituals, counting prayers, and stockpiling good works in hopes that the "naughty and nice" scale will tip in our favor. When will we realize that heaven is not a reward, it is a gift? But no matter what we do, truth is still there, waiting to be acknowledged.

> Truth is incontrovertible. Panic may resent it; ignorance may deride it; malice may distort it; but there it is.
>
> —Winston Churchill

MOI? SELF-CENTERED?

I recall reading an article when I was in my thirties, written by a psychiatrist who stated that overly sensitive people are self-centered. He explained that when such individuals are chronically offended, it is because their world centers on them, what happens to them, and their feelings. He challenged his readers to take note of how many times "I," "me," and "my" are used in conversations (this included self-talk).

I recall I was initially offended by the psychiatrist's statement. Me? Self-centered? I'm one of the most unselfish people I know. I'm always doing things for others!

As I struggled honestly with his statements, however, I realized that I *was* self-centered. I had a chronic case of "I" trouble. In almost every situation, "I" was the center of my concern. "I" was hurt, "I" was treated unfairly, "I" was misunderstood, "I" disagreed, "I" would never have said or done that, and "I" would have done it differently...I, I, I. My entire thought world system revolved around me.

It became apparent that I needed to think less about me and my feelings and more about others—where they were coming from and what they were feeling. When I started being honest with myself, I had to admit that most of the "unselfish" things I did for others were actually selfish. Yes, I wanted to help them, but my primary joy came from feeling good about myself. I wanted and needed the praise of others. And the best way to get it was to always be doing something for others, even if it meant sacrificing precious time with my husband and children. That way I could say to myself, *See what a good person I am!*

Through my pursuit of honesty, I asked God to help me develop a genuine love and concern for others. Guess what? My self-centeredness lessened and I began to develop a proper self-esteem.

We hear and read much about the need for a positive self-image, but what we need is a proper self-image. When we do wrong, we should feel bad! Our guilt can be used as a tool to get us back on the right track. As our proper self-image develops, we will develop more confidence to scrutinize ourselves honestly.

Once I discovered that I wouldn't crumble from my own scrutiny, I was freed from the need to appear perfect. I relaxed and became more open and transparent with others without fear that my flaws might be seen. I discovered that when I accepted myself, others accepted me. They related more to my humanness than to my prior façade of "perfection." My credibility grew—not only with others but with myself.

Of all that is involved in the development of good character and a strong, healthy self-esteem, I believe the most important is a sincere desire to please God. This desire leads one to the foot of God's throne and to obedience. Only when we walk with God in obedience can we taste the fruit of His promises.

> The promises of God are of no value to us until, through obedience, we come to understand the nature of God. We may read some things in the Bible every day for a year and they may mean nothing to us. Then, because we have been obedient to God in some small detail, we suddenly see what God means and His nature is instantly opened up to us.
>
> —Oswald Chambers, *My Utmost for His Highest*

> ...our goal is to please him (2 Corinthians 5:9).

WHAT IF...?

Just as self-centered thoughts do not please God, neither do anxious and fearful thoughts.

When our children were small, I sometimes accompanied my husband on business trips required in our retail/wholesale business. I wanted to go and was a great help to him, but I suffered anxiety over leaving the children.

What if they get sick? What if they have an accident? What if the house catches on fire? I conjured up all kinds of horrible things that could happen while I wasn't there. It didn't matter that we had competent, mature babysitters, a telephone on the premises, and lived near a hospital. I worried anyway.

CHANGING THE "WHAT IF?" PROGRAMS

Then something happened that gave me power to go in the opposite direction. After overdoing it with yard work one day, I found myself in my chiropractor's office. Because I had not gone in promptly for an adjustment, that area in my back was particularly tender. The chiropractor positioned me for manipulation and instructed me to relax. Because that area was so painful, I feared the adjustment might hurt and I couldn't relax. After a couple of unsuccessful attempts, he said, "Wiggle the toes on your right foot." When I wiggled my toes, he made the adjustment—without pain.

"Why did I have to wiggle my toes?" I asked.

"When you concentrated on wiggling your toes," he explained, "your focus shifted from your pain to your toes. You relaxed and I could make the adjustment."

Driving home, I thought, Why wouldn't the "wiggle your toes" principle work in other areas?

I had read or heard somewhere that worry is merely negative imagination. Could I break the chain of worry by substituting positive imagination for the negative? When we left on our next trip and the old negative thought patterns began to play, I changed tactics. I substituted positive "what ifs" for the usual negatives.

What if, while we are gone, the babysitter is watching the children playing in the front yard and a kind white-haired gentleman walks by and stops to chat with them? He is a lonely widower with no children nor grandchildren of his own. Our kids really take to him. The babysitter carefully observes him and decides he's just a harmless, kind, lonely old man who loves children. He chats with them for a while and then resumes his walk.

I build this scenario to the point that when we return home, we become friends with the kind old man and adopt him into our family circle. Several years later, he dies and leaves a fortune to our children. (And we had thought he was penniless!) Our children's college education was secured. Our son became a surgeon and our daughter an attorney.

Wait a minute, my logical mind interjects. *This is a stupid story! Just because you are gone on a business trip, you think that's going to hap-*

pen? Not likely! But I, now knowing that I have the power to wiggle my mental toes and break the negative focus, reply, *That's true. But neither is it likely that my house is going to burn down just because I am gone.*

After our second trip, I was free of the negative worries—forever. I received more than a manipulation that freed me from physical pain that day at the chiropractor's office. I discovered a method of attitude adjustment that freed me from a lifetime of mental and emotional pain.

Chapter Eighteen

Step Three: Gratitude

Thus far we have covered two of the three steps necessary to become an overcomer—forgiveness (with its three facets) and responsibility for our thoughts and actions. Gratitude is the third step. Omit it and we cannot complete our journey. Gratitude protects us from following the tempting siren call of self-pity into the quagmire of quicksand. And without gratitude we can never know joy.

> Gratitude is not only the greatest of virtues, but the parent of all the others.
>
> —Cicero

> Gratitude is the fairest blossom which springs from the soul.
>
> —Henry Ward Beecher

THE KEY TO GRATITUDE

"But how can I be grateful when I have so many problems?" you ask. "And who doesn't want to feel grateful all the time? It's hard when worries press in upon me from every side, and I feel like the only light at the end of the tunnel really is the proverbial freight train. Believe me, I would love to enter into that elusive state of gratitude, but sometimes the door is shut tight. What do I do then?"

Trust. "Trust in the LORD with all your heart; do not depend on your own understanding" (Proverbs 3:5). Trust is the golden key that unlocks the door of gratitude. But can we really lean completely on God and trust Him? We've already seen that we can't put any weight on our own understanding—we believe a lie too easily. We believe the lies we tell ourselves and the lies that others tell us.

On an earthly level, we want to trust people, but first we need to know that they are trustworthy. How many people do you trust completely—people to whom you would entrust all of your earthly possessions, even your very life? You are fortunate if you can name more than two or three people.

Why do you trust them? Because they have integrity—and they have a good track record.

They have kept every promise they made to you. Or at least they have tried.

God is that kind of friend. There are many powerful descriptions of God in Scripture—good, wise, loving, patient, just, righteous, perfect, holy. There is another description, however, that you may not have considered.

> This truth gives them confidence that they have eternal life, which God—who does not lie—promised them before the world began (Titus 1:2).

Why can't God lie? I asked myself after first reading that verse. *He can do anything He wants—He's God!*

Later, I contemplated Isaiah 43:25: "I—yes, I alone—will blot out your sins for my own sake and will never think of them again."

I marveled at a love so strong that it could not only forgive a person of his or her sins, but also never bring them up again! I had been forgiven by friends for wrongs I had done, but sometimes they reminded me of my past offenses—to either humiliate me or to make me feel obligated.

Why would God make and keep such a promise? Four little words, tucked away in the middle of that verse, answer this question: "for my own sake."

What a strange phrase! I thought, *I wonder what it means?*

Later that day, I overheard a conversation between two men discussing a mutual friend. "One thing I appreciate about Jim is his integrity. When he says he'll do something, I don't ever have to worry about it—it's as good as done. He always keeps his word."

That's it! I thought, recalling the phrase in Isaiah— "for my own sake." *God will keep every promise He makes—not because of who we are, but because of who He is. And that is why God cannot lie.*

God doesn't have integrity—God *is* integrity. He is the author of truth. When He makes a promise, it's as good as done. His consistency, based on who He is, will never be affected by our moods, our circumstances, or our actions. God is a holy and just God who will always keep His word. And for that assurance, our every breath should be one of undying gratitude.

HOW TO BECOME MORE GRATEFUL

We set the stage for misery when we ignore our blessings. Show me a person who is consistently unhappy and I'll show you a person who is consistently ungrateful.

Tip #1: Don't compare yourself or your circumstances with others. The person who plays the comparison game will never be happy. There will always be someone around who is smarter, better looking, richer, and more talented. Many survivors are plagued by an inferiority complex, which will surface in one of two ways. They either have a competitive need to outdo every one around them to prove their own value, or they undervalue themselves and insist that the talents they possess are inferior. Both attitudes are incorrect. For many years I suffered from inferiority feelings that match those of the second type—and sometimes I still struggle.

Both perceptions can be corrected when we focus on the truth about our value. Our worth lies not in what we do but in who we are. We are beloved children of God—daughters and sons of the King. There is no greater rank. We have "already arrived." We can't do one thing to motivate our heavenly Father to love us any more than He already does. When we accept this truth, we won't feel the need to prove our worth to God or anyone else—especially ourselves.

Sometimes we are dissatisfied because others seem to have more and better possessions. We would be content if only we had a bigger house, nicer clothes, a fancier car, smarter children, a more thoughtful husband—then we would be happy. But how do we know when enough is enough? Regardless of how much you have, you can still be grateful—grateful that you have life, that God loves you, grateful for the specific things God has already given you, grateful in all circumstances!

> I have learned how to be content with whatever I have (Philippians 4:11).

Since we have a choice as to whether we will be content or discontented, doesn't it make sense to choose the attitude that will create joy? Discontentment only leads to more pain—such as envy and greed. Did you know that we are never more like Satan than when we envy? It was because of envy that Satan rebelled against God.

Besides, things may not always be as they appear. The woman you may at this moment be envying may have her own secret desires to live your life. A statement printed at the top of a note I received from a friend one day says it well: "The grass that appears greener on the other side may be only Astroturf."

Conclusion: If we don't compare ourselves with others we are more able to be grateful.

Tip #2: Reprogram your attitude. The only real handicap in life is a bad attitude. Remember how I retrained my mental muscles to reject critical thoughts of my husband? Remember how when a critical, faultfinding thought popped into my mind, I deliberately looked for ten positive attributes in my husband? The same exercise routine can be used to build gratitude. Stop complaining, and strengthen your gratitude muscles. For each complaint your mind focuses upon, wiggle your mental toes and look for ten blessings. This should be easy since we have countless more blessings than disadvantages. Then thank God for each blessing.

Conclusion: If we look for blessings, we will be too busy to complain.

Tip #3: Choose the proper residence for your mind. "Fix your thoughts on what is true, and honorable, and right, and pure, and lovely, and admirable. Think about things that are excellent and worthy of praise" (Philippians 4:8).

How could the apostle Paul, as he sat in a dungeon, tell us to be thankful regardless of our circumstances? Because he knew from experience that when we give thanks in every situation, every situation becomes bearable. Besides, his body may have been in a dungeon, but his mind didn't dwell there.

If you decided to build a new home, and you could build it any place you wanted, would you build it in the middle of the city dump? Then why would you allow the most beautiful possession you own to reside there? Since the mind is a terrible thing to waste, doesn't it deserve to dwell in a healthy and beautiful residence instead of a wasteland? If you are currently dwelling in the dumps, move. It's a stinky, miserable place that results in "stinkin' thinkin'"—a mind-set that you and your family and friends should not be expected to endure. Move your mind to a brighter place that focuses on good things, not the bad, and practice gratitude. For without gratitude, your life will remain miserable even though you move into a mansion.

Conclusion: If you want to develop an attitude of gratitude, then house your mind in pleasant thoughts.

Tip #4: Learn to "be thankful in all circumstances" (1 Thessalonians 5:18). I recall an incident that occurred right after I first set out to develop an "attitude of gratitude." I was running behind schedule one morning, as usual. After loading my car with what I needed for a day of busy activities, I slammed the car door shut, started the engine, and was backing out of the garage when it happened: the zipper in my slacks broke.

A month earlier I would have come unglued. "Oh, great! This is going to be a lousy day!" I would have fumed and fretted, wasting valuable energy that was needed for a busy day.

However, I was determined to live out Paul's admonition to "give thanks in every situation."

I stopped the engine, took a deep breath, and thought, *There's got to be something in this situation for which I can be thankful.* I looked for reasons to be thankful, and guess what? I found them.

As I dashed inside to change, I whispered, "Thank you, Lord, that I picked up my other dressy pair of slacks from the cleaners yesterday. And thank you that my zipper broke at this moment instead of later this morning. And thank you that it was my zipper that broke and not my ankle."

It took only a few minutes to change and I was back on the road. The most important change I made that morning, however, was not my change of clothes, but my change in attitude. I changed a grumpy attitude into a grateful one. It was my choice.

Conclusion: We don't have to let unwanted circumstances control our behavior. We can find blessings in every situation.

If you work each day on the above steps, before you know it, your complaints will cease and you will enjoy life as a grateful person.

JOY—A CHOSEN FRUIT

My friend Dr. Curt Brannan related an incident that occurred during one of his visits to a local rest home when he was our pastor in Ojai, California. One of the inhabitants there, named Charlie, was a delightful man who was confined to a wheelchair. As he zipped around the facility, Charlie was always happy, spreading sunshine wherever he went. Curt knew he experienced persistent pain and marveled at Charlie's consistent thoughtfulness and cheery attitude.

One day Curt asked him, "Charlie, why are you so cheerful and happy all of the time?"

Charlie grinned and answered, "Because that's the way I want to be."

> I've noticed that people are generally about as happy as they make up their minds to be.
>
> —Abraham Lincoln

> A cheerful heart is good medicine, but a broken spirit saps a person's strength (Proverbs 17:22).

Peter Haile writes in his book *The Difference God Makes— Living as if God Matters*:

> If we have been born again, we have been born of God's Spirit; we have been infused with his very life; we have been made partners of the divine nature; we are God's heirs, God's offspring. It is now

> our nature to want to do what God wants us to do. This was brought home to me once by a friend who said, "When I'm tempted, I stop to remember that a Christian can do whatever he wants to do."
>
> I replied, "Now wait a minute. I thought that's just what a Christian couldn't do."
>
> And then he said to me, "Do you want to be unloving? Do you want to be selfish? Do you want to be impure?"
>
> Immediately I knew that what he had said was true. I did not want to be selfish; in fact, it was the last thing I wanted to be.

As ransomed children of the King, the purest desire of our heart is to walk closely with Christ and bear evidence that with His help we can do anything we want! We want to love, not hate, forgive, not resent, and trust, not fear. And we *can* do all these things. Christ paid for our freedom and we can overcome anything! Such good news bears repeating: Christ paid for our freedom! We are free! Talk about joy!

"If that don't light your fire," says my friend Beth Christensen, "then your wood's wet!"

THE PROOF OF THE PUDDING IS IN THE EATING

Are these just empty words written in a book by a writer because they fit in with the subject of overcoming versus merely surviving? Is the author really an overcomer?

You decide.

- I no longer suffer from nightmares about my father.
- I watch court scenes on television and participate as an objective juror without reliving the old negative feelings of anger and shame I felt during Dad's trial.
- While I am satisfied that my father served time in prison for his crime against my mother, I feel compassion when I think of him and his wasted life.
- My father was wrong in all that he did that caused my family and me pain, but I forgave him. I haven't the slightest residue of anger toward him. I am free of resentment and bitterness.
- I speak of my father, not with disdain or a rise in blood pressure, but in a respectful, calm, and sad manner.
- I do not blame my father for my shortcomings, my weaknesses, nor my failures. I assume full responsibility for all of my choices in life.

- I refuse to entertain thoughts of self-pity, regardless of what happens in life. I have obliterated "Why me?" from my mental vocabulary. Instead, I ask, "Why not me? God's grace is sufficient to help me in any situation." I have changed my "why?" to "how?" "How, Lord, can You be honored in this situation?"

> Nothing robs one's strength and vitality so much as self-absorption. There is no greater waste of time than self-pity, pre-occupation with self; it fragments and dissipates that which you want to be about.
>
> —Tim Hansel, *You Gotta Keep Dancin'*

Photographs of my father holding us children when we were little, as well as photos of his second family, are included on our family photo wall. Are they there because he is a great example of fatherhood? No. They are there because he is my father. They are there to serve as evidence that each of Dad's children—my brother, my sister, and I— have forgiven him.

When a friend of mine mentioned to someone that my father's pictures are on our photo wall, the other person's response was, "That's sick!"

But is it? Including my father's photos on our wall evidences another truth. Not only do I hold no resentment toward him, neither am I burdened with feelings of shame. I don't live in fear that someone might find out about the wrong choices my father made. Truth is the key that unlocks the door to shame. I use this key as an opportunity to show that, with God's help, our right choices can overcome the harm done by the wrong choices of others. It is also an opportunity to point out the importance of our making the right choices, since they always affect those around us. So, am I sick, or am I healthy?

I thank God for what He has helped me to become through my negative experiences. Of course, I am not thankful *for* my father's abuse. *That* would be sick! But I am thankful that the evil committed by my father is being overcome by the good that God is able to accomplish in the lives of my siblings and myself.

I thank God for all blessings—not just on Thanksgiving Day, but every day. Because, like Charlie in the rest home, "That's the way I want to be!" Always grateful—and joyful.

Chapter Nineteen

Joy in Hard Times

> A bird doesn't sing because he has an answer—he sings because he has a song.
> —Joan Anglund

Choosing joy will provide new strength and vigor, not only for today but also for the future—when the rough times come. And they will. We would be wise to get mentally prepared, as did Habakkuk.

> Even though the fig trees have no blossoms, and there are no grapes on the vines; even though the olive crop fails, and the fields lie empty and barren; even though the flocks die in the fields, and the cattle barns are empty, yet I will rejoice in the Lord! I will be joyful in the God of my salvation! (Habakkuk 3:17-18)

Why does Habakkuk determine to rejoice in such dire circumstances should they come? Because, regardless of our shifting sands of circumstance, God is our constant source of strength.

"The Sovereign LORD is my strength! He makes me as surefooted as a deer, able to tread upon the heights" (Habakkuk 3:19). Habakkuk knows that God will lead him to higher pastures of hope and provide him stability that will help him to dig his heels in and avoid sliding into the bleak valley of despondency below.

When the California recession drove Jerry and me from our beautiful home in Oakhurst, California, it completely changed the direction of our lives. We had struggled for several years to make payments on our two-acre parcel in the mountains near beautiful Yosemite National Park, and had designed and built what we thought would be our retirement home. We had walked through the wooded terrain, laying the lines for our dream home to catch the perfect view of the valley below and the snow-covered mountains beyond. Before we even broke ground, I planted daffodil bulbs on each side of the deer path that led downhill through the gnarled Manzanita trees, oaks, and pines to the seasonal creek and waterfall below. When finished and furnished, our home was even more beautiful than we had hoped. But the recession was worsening.

One by one we saw businesses flee California and relocate their businesses to other states. One close friend urged us to do the same. "Don't wait until it's too late," he warned. Some had already waited too long and had lost everything, including their home. But we refused to acknowledge the density of the dark clouds on the economy's horizon.

"California is our home—how can we leave it?" we asked each other. "Besides, California has weathered recessions before—it will turn around soon."

But it didn't. We ran out of money before the recession ran out of breath. We not only lost our business but every penny we had saved and invested for our retirement. And we were deep in debt.

But I prepared myself to let go. Even as I dug and developed sixteen beds for my favorite roses, lovingly transported from the Ojai Valley where we had previously lived, I recall thinking, *I may not get to enjoy this rose garden very long—but someone will.* I reminded myself often of something Corrie ten Boom had written about hanging onto things in life loosely because it hurt too much when God had to pry her fingers loose.

Three-and-a-half years after moving into our home, we closed its doors and sadly turned over the keys to a property management firm to lease, since we had been unable to sell it. We were moving to the deserts of Arizona. At an age when we had hoped to be in a position to retire, we had to start all over again in a strange land, broke and heavyhearted. But before we left, I again prepared myself. As I stood looking out over the valley from our bay window in the breakfast nook off our country kitchen, I made a decision.

When I am living in the middle of the desert—a place I always said I would never live—and I am in my tiny apartment kitchen with no windows, I will not long for the beauty of this oak-framed garden window above my sink where I watch the deer walk to the creek below, nor the openness of this nook that allows the awesomeness of nature to filter through its glass walls. Nor will I covet the storage space in these wall-to-wall cabinets. I will not complain, nor will I make myself miserable by comparing what I don't have with what I once had. I will thank God for this short chapter of life and its beautiful memories. I will thank Him daily for that little apartment, the brevity of the time it will take to clean it, and for all of my blessings, beginning with my loving, hardworking husband and the good health that enables us to again labor fulltime in the work force—at sixty years of age. I will trust my present and future circumstances to my Lord, who has never failed me.

And that's exactly what happened.

> Wise men never sit and wail their loss, but cheerily seek how to redress their harms.
>
> —William Shakespeare

I believe my past losses taught me to let go quickly. Because I had to leave my home and everything dear to me at the age of nineteen, I was better prepared for future losses. Through experience, I learned that things are temporary but God's love is permanent.

It was hard for Jerry to step over the ashes of our California business, leave the mountain home that he had worked so hard on to the care of tenants because we could not sell it, and submit to a new economic harness by working for strangers in the desert of Arizona. Those first several years were difficult. We rarely saw each other. I worked at night at a local hospital and he worked during the day as an estimator for a commercial glass company.

But God did not abandon us in the desert. With the help of a young partner, Jerry started another commercial glass business which flourished and steadily grew. I was able to take early retirement and pursue my writing and speaking. After paying off old debts, we bought a two story lakefront home. Jerry found a used eighteen-foot pontoon boat and we began to relax again as we enjoyed romantic moonlit nights cruising around the lake. We thanked God for our blessings as we watched the ducks swim lazily in our cove. But we never took the beauty for granted, nor did we sink our roots into its soil. We knew it was temporary. We understood that whether we left our new haven by choice one day, or if we were forced to leave and live out our lives in a cozy shack due to another unexpected financial reversal, we were not going to worry about it—we trusted our Lord. We had already learned that far more important than the kind of house one lives in is the kind of attitude that lives within the house.

It is imperative that each of us prepares for the hard times ahead. We need to think about what we are unwilling to give up. Is it our independence, our status, our health, home, child, or mate? It is our nature to want to dig our heels in and, with arms crossed like a stubborn child, cry, "No, Lord! Don't let this happen! I could not handle it!" But our fingers will bleed when they are pried loose from that which we are unwilling to release, and a rip will appear in our heart through which our joy will escape.

In 1988 I was diagnosed with endometrial cancer and faced immediate surgery. The doctors believed the cancer had spread into the lymph glands and were certain I would require additional treatment. I was at peace, but Jerry was devastated. "God has to let you survive. He knows I can't live without you!" he said the night before my surgery, eyes tearing.

"The Lord doesn't know any such thing!" I said gently. "You don't live for Kitty Chappell—you live for God! You can live without me, but you can't live without Him. You must let me go whether or not I survive."

The next morning when I arose, he had been up for hours, praying. His eyes glowed as he took my hands and said, "I did it—I let you go! I will trust the Lord whatever happens, for I know He will be with me." I faced my surgery that morning free of concern, for Jerry and I as a team had placed ourselves in God's hands. The cancer was intact and surgery removed it all.

I believe Jerry's ability to face and accept my mortality prepared him for the day when he had to face and accept his own. In October of 2000, Jerry was diagnosed with cancer—non-Hodgkin's lymphoma. He told me the news hit him hard. For over an hour he just drove around, wondering how he was going to tell me, and asking God, "Why me, Lord?" By the time he arrived home, however, he had accepted it.

He underwent a series of successful radiation treatments in good spirits. He did well for three years, returning only for routine blood work, scans, and checkups.

But in 2003 the cancer returned with a vengeance. In six months, between scans, a huge tumor developed near his apex—too close to his heart to operate. Jerry underwent several rounds of chemotherapy, but never missed a day at the office. He'd rise early, drive to a nearby city where he underwent his infusions, eat a restaurant breakfast, and then drive straight to his office where he worked the rest of the day.

The tumor shrank somewhat, but not enough. He patiently endured another round of chemo. Through it all, his spirit was dauntless. His smile and sense of humor lit up the offices where he went for treatment, scans, and workups.

One day someone asked "How can you be so cheerful through all of this?"

"Because I'm in a win-win situation—either all of this treatment will cure me or I'll go home to heaven where I won't need it." He grinned and then added, "I can't lose for winning."

Yes, Jerry was going through hard times—but he never lost his joy.

> Don't be dejected and sad, for the joy of the LORD is your strength (Nehemiah 8:10).

When we accept the bottom line, we can live on the top—where joy dwells. When we trust our future to God, think of and accept the absolute worst that can happen, what is there left to fear?

Fear knocked at the door.
Faith answered.
No one was there.

As we walk through life, reality teaches us that everything we have, regardless of our precautions, can be taken from us. Stocks crash, banks fail, economies collapse, investments turn sour—tornadoes, cyclones, fires, and flood can destroy our home and everything in it. Even our loved ones can be taken from us through a plane crash, an automobile accident, a sniper's bullet, or a terminal disease.

Jerry and I knew that all too well. He lost his father, two brothers, and a brother-in-law to cancer. I lost my maternal grandfather and two step-grandfathers to cancer. I knew I could also lose my Jerry—and that would break my heart. But I also believed that should that happen, my joy in the Lord would remain intact. I would hurt, yes, but life would not be over for me no matter how much I missed Jerry. God would be there again to take my heart and mend it with His loving hands—just as He had always done.

So far as God is concerned, if we belong to Him, we *can* overcome all of these things—with His help. In fact, He expects us to overcome because of who we are. And *we* should expect it!

> But you belong to God, my dear children. You have already won a victory..., because the Spirit who lives in you is greater than the spirit who lives in the world (1 John 4:4).

> No, despite all these things, overwhelming victory is ours through Christ, who loved us. And I am convinced that nothing can ever separate us from God's love. Neither death nor life, neither angels nor demons, neither our fears for today nor our worries about tomorrow—not even the powers of hell can separate us from God's love (Romans 8:37-39).

Jerry planned to retire in December of 2005 and build a single-story home he had just designed, but the cancer suddenly spread to his lungs. Following a two-week hospitalization, and a valiant short battle, my sweet Jerry went home to be with the Lord in May of that year. Though my belief and trust in God were intact, my feelings weren't. The gaping wound left in my heart when Jerry was ripped from it felt as though it would never heal. The poem below best expresses those feelings.

WHEN I HURT, LORD
Kitty Chappell

When I hurt, Lord, and fear my pain will slay me
As I fight my unwanted flood of circumstances;
When life's stormy waters would pull me under
As they lash relentlessly at my very foundation,
Lift me up, Lord.

When the strongest hope I have is to but awaken
From a bad dream and see life as I'd like it to be,
But cries from my soul shout the pain of reality
In my ears, and my eyes see things as they are,
Help me trust, Lord.

When my soul is hollow with hurt and I feel fragile
And wonder why, when yesterday I felt so strong;
When I fear I will shatter into a million pieces
Unless You embrace me with Your arms of love,
Hold me together, Lord,
until I am mended.

> Do not be afraid, for I have ransomed you. I have called you by name; you are mine. When you go through deep waters and great trouble, I will be with you. When you go through rivers of difficulty, you will not drown!...For I am the LORD, your God...your Savior...you are pre-

> cious to me. You are honored, and I love you.
>
> —Taken from Isaiah 43

God never meant for the pain in our heart to be more than temporary. His word validates that truth.

> And now, dear brothers and sisters, we want you to know what will happen to the believers who have died so you will not grieve like people who have no hope. For since we believe that Jesus died and was raised to life again, we also believe that when Jesus returns, God will bring back with him the believers who have died (1 Thessalonians 4:13-14).

It has been over two years now and my heart is whole again—healed by God just as I had believed. From the moment God welcomed Jerry with open arms into heaven, He embraced me with His love and wisdom. I learned quickly that when I focused on where Jerry *is* and not on where he *isn't,* my pain subsided. Shifting the focus from my pain to Jerry's joy helped me avoid self-pity which would have prolonged my pain and hindered the healing process. The old saying, "If you truly love someone, you will want what is best for them, even if it's not what you want" helped me with this focus. How many times have I looked up to heaven and whispered through tears, "Honey, I am *so* happy for you—you have truly 'escaped the tempter's snare.'"

Yes, we can overcome the deepest heartaches—and with our joy intact.

> You will live in joy and peace. The mountains and hills will burst into song, and the trees of the field will clap their hands (Isaiah 55:12).

Once again God proved in my life there can be joy in the hard times. We will never be robbed of that joy, no matter how hard the circumstances, if we choose to live our lives for God and not for ourselves. We can choose joy or self-pity, forgiveness or bitterness, life or death—but only we can make those choices.

> Today I have given you the choice between life and death, between blessings and curses. Now I call on heaven and earth to witness the choice you make. Oh, that you would choose life, so that you and your descendants might live! You can make this choice by loving the LORD your God, obeying him, and committing yourself firmly to him. This is the key to your life (Deuteronomy 30:19-20).